The Trail to Wholeness
Copyright © 2025 by Robert Yadon

ISBN (Paperback): 979-8-9930596-0-0

Published by Robert Yadon

Cover design by Robert Yadon

Disclaimer: This book is for informational and inspirational purposes only. It is not intended as a substitute for professional medical or psychological advice, diagnosis, or treatment. Readers dealing with trauma, PTSD, or depression should seek the guidance of a licensed healthcare professional.

Printed in the United States of America

Dedication Page

For the men who are still walking wounded.
For the fathers who wonder if they are enough.
For the brothers who carry silent battles.
This trail is for you.

"Most of us don't need more advice. We need more friends. Men who will walk beside us—not to fix us, but just to keep going together."

Author's Note / Preface

I didn't set out to write a book; I set out to survive. For years, I carried wounds that no one could see: the aftermath of trauma, the weight of a school shooting I survived, and the quiet battles with depression and PTSD that crept into every corner of my life. Like many men, I pushed it down, put on the mask, and tried to keep moving.

What I didn't realize was that silence was slowly undoing me.

This book is both a story and a field guide. It's about how nature, adventure, and brotherhood can heal what isolation breaks. It's about the moments when I nearly gave up and the unexpected places where I found hope again.

If you are carrying your own invisible weight, I want you to know you're not alone. There is a way forward, and there is life beyond survival. This is the map I wish someone had handed me years ago. My hope is that it becomes a trail marker for you, too.

— Robert Yadon

The Trail to Wholeness: A Survival Guide for Men Facing Stress, Loneliness, and the Call of the Wild

by R L YADON

Table of Contents

Introduction: The Trail to Wholeness

There's a silent epidemic sweeping through men's lives. It doesn't always make the headlines or show up in dramatic, obvious ways. Instead, it stays quietly beneath the surface of our daily routines, our hard-won achievements, and the carefully constructed facades we present to the world. It is the quiet desperation of the modern man, a struggle carried in solitude, often hidden from our partners, our children, and even from ourselves.

This wasn't always the story of manhood. For generations, the path, while often difficult, was at least clear. A man's worth was tied to a steady job, a home, and the family he provided for. These were tangible goalposts. But in the last few decades, those goalposts have shifted, rusted, or collapsed altogether. The promise that hard work and stoic endurance would lead to a life of fulfillment has revealed itself to be a hollow one for many, if not most, men. We were given a map to a world that no longer exists, and we are now left navigating a new, more complex terrain with no guide, feeling the pressure to be providers in a precarious economy, to be protectors in a world that feels unsafe, and to be emotionally present partners and fathers without ever being taught how.

This epidemic has many faces. It's the constant, quiet hum that often begins in boyhood, a persistent whisper that echoes in the back of our minds with a single, corrosive message: "you're not good enough". It's a feeling of inherent inadequacy that no amount of success or external validation seems to silence. It's the suffocating, invisible weight of expectations, the unspoken mandate to always be the provider, to be the protector, to have it all figured out, even, and especially, when we feel utterly and completely lost inside. It's a weight familiar to any man who has ever felt the silent pressure to be the unshakable pillar for his family, terrified of what might happen if he admits to having cracks in his own foundation.

It's also the pervasive, aching loneliness that can creep in, even when we are in a crowded room, even when we are surrounded by people who love us. It's the profound sense of disconnection that comes from a lifetime of surface-level conversations, a world of handshakes and head-nods where true, authentic connection feels like a foreign language. And finally, it's the unspoken pain of trauma, depression, and anxiety that so many of us carry in absolute silence, buried under the deeply ingrained belief that to admit struggle is to admit weakness, a price that feels far too high to pay.

I know this hum. I know this weight. I know this silence. I don't just know it from research or observation. I live it. For years, I wore the armor that society hands to so many of us boys. I was the sensitive kid who quickly learned that the safest way to navigate the world was to hide his feelings, to build a wall around his heart. I became a young father at eighteen, drowning in a sea of shame and judgment, trying desperately to project an image of a man who had it all under control when, in reality, I was terrified and lost. I was the Emergency Medical Technician who, call after horrific call, learned to compartmentalize trauma, to pack it away in neat little boxes in my mind, until the day those boxes began to splinter and break, threatening to take me down with them. I was the man who chased financial success with a relentless, punishing fervor, believing that if I could just earn enough, I could finally prove my worth to the world and to myself, only to find myself completely hollowed out by the grind, and still broke. Even when my life is full, when I am surrounded by colleagues, students, and family, I often feel deeply and profoundly lonely, convinced that needing others was a weakness I couldn't afford to show. I truly and fully believed that strength meant enduring my burdens silently, that vulnerability was a dangerous liability, and that my ultimate worth as a man was directly tied to how well I could tough it out all by myself.

But here is the hard-won truth that I've had to learn: that kind of strength? It will kill you. Not with a bang, but with a slow, insidious bleed. It is a false strength that drains you over years of accumulated silence, unspoken resentments, and buried pain. It eats away at your relationships from the inside out, creating a distance between you and the people you love most. It chips away at your self-worth until you feel like a ghost in your own life.

This book is for the men who are tired of that silence. It's for the men who can feel the cracks forming in their own armor, who are exhausted by the relentless grind, who yearn for real, authentic connection, and who have a nagging suspicion deep in their gut that there must be a different, better way to be strong. My own journey out of that silence has been a long and winding trail. I didn't have a single, dramatic moment of revelation. I already knew I was lonely and that I was struggling with my mental health. A trip to Peru, which I will discuss in Chapter 6, didn't begin my healing, but it certainly amplified everything. The physical and mental challenge of that adventure became a crucible that intensified my awareness of my own struggles, while at the same time, showing me the profound and life-saving power of true brotherhood.

After that trip, I threw myself into a new physical discipline, working out daily with renewed vigor. Yet, the true catalyst that finally pushed me to start speaking my truth, to write this book, and to come out of my shell came not from a moment of triumph, but from a moment of profound disappointment. I was overlooked for a potential job swap at work; a position my principal had previously assured me she would support me in pursuing it if it became available. To then discover that the opening had been filled without a single word that it had become available was the final straw. That feeling of being unseen, of having my efforts and my potential completely dismissed, ignited a fire within me. In that moment, I realized a fundamental truth: if I wanted to be seen, if I wanted my life to have meaning, I had to stop waiting for others to give me permission. I had to speak up as an advocate for myself. I am not mad or hold any negative feelings towards my principal, and definitely not towards the individual that was hired. Honestly, she seems awesome and very good at what she does. She was a great choice for the position, however, that feeling of being overlooked and invisible to not have been given a fair chance was the final nail in the coffin.

I didn't decide to write this book because I had all the answers. I wrote it because I didn't. I was tired of being the guy who pretended he was okay when he wasn't, the man nodding along in conversations while a storm raged inside. And I realized I wasn't the only one. Everywhere I looked, in the teacher's lounge, on the sidelines of my kids' soccer games, in the quiet nods from old friends, I saw men carrying the same invisible burdens, hiding behind the same façade I had perfected. Writing became my way of breaking the silence, of holding up a lantern in the fog and saying, 'I see you." I'm walking this trail too.'

This book is a small part of my story, yes. But it is also our story. It is for you, not for me. It is a deep dive into the silent crisis of men's mental health, PTSD, depression, and loneliness, but it is grounded not just in my personal experiences. It is also grounded in the latest research and insights into what truly helps men heal, connect, and thrive. I am not famous, nor am I some hardcore influencer seeking likes. I am just a regular guy, a husband, a father, and a teacher, trying my best to find my way.

Together, on this trail, we will explore:

- "Cracks in the Armor": We will begin by examining how our early life experiences and the immense pressures of society shape our understanding of manhood, often leading to the deep-seated feelings of inadequacy and shame that so many of us carry.

- "Trauma in the Rearview": We will look honestly at the insidious ways that cumulative trauma, especially in high-stress roles, can linger in our nervous systems and manifest in our daily lives, and we will confront the question of why we as men so often resist seeking the help we desperately need.

- "The Weight of Ghosts: A Man's Guide to Grief and Loss": We will confront the wound of loss, exploring how the unspoken script for male grief, to be the rock, to manage logistics, to grieve in silence, forces us to carry our heaviest burdens alone. Through personal stories of cumulative loss, we will give a name to the feeling of being "lost to the world you grew up in" and find a way to carry our ghosts with honor.

- "Buried by the Grind": We will tackle the unspoken pressure of financial stress and its corrosive effect on a man's identity and self-worth, and we will learn how to redefine "enough" to build a life of meaning, not just a life of endless pursuit.

- "Beyond the Grind": We will offer a direct critique of the toxic myths of hustle culture and its detrimental effects on our well-being, focusing instead on building sustainable habits, firm boundaries, and embracing the essential role of rest in preventing burnout.

- "Brotherhood in the Wild": We will confront the alarming male loneliness epidemic and explore the life-saving power of authentic male friendships, particularly those forged through the quiet power of shared presence and vulnerability in the outdoors.

- "Sustaining Brotherhood": We will bridge the gap between knowing we need brotherhood and the brutal truth of maintaining it in our chaotic adult lives.

- "Adventure as a Way of Life": We will discover how small, accessible "microadventures" can become powerful tools for mental resets, emotional regulation, and fostering deep connections with our families and with ourselves.

- "The Father Wound": We will turn inward to explore how our inherited emotional patterns impact our own parenting, and we will learn how to consciously break these generational cycles to become the more present, emotionally available fathers our children deserve.

- "Marriage, Distance, and the Invisible Load": We will navigate the unique challenges that men face in modern relationships, giving a name to the unspoken burdens we carry and learning strategies to foster deeper intimacy and a true sense of shared partnership.

- "Finding North: The Unspoken Power of Mentors and Role Models": We will explore how positive male role models can help men redefine strength and vulnerability, providing a map for a healthier, more integrated masculinity.

- "A New Kind of Strong": We will work toward a powerful redefinition of masculinity, one that challenges the outdated ideals of stoicism and instead includes vulnerability, emotional intelligence, and authentic connection as the true indicators of a man's strength.

- "Integration – The Adventure of Becoming Whole Again": Finally, we will come to understand that healing is not a fixed destination or a "fix," but an ongoing, lifelong journey of pulling all the threads of your life together, your past pain, your resilience, your failures, and your wins and letting them coexist without the heavy burden of shame.

This is not a book of quick fixes or easy answers. It is a book about showing up. Showing up for yourself. For your family. For your friends. It is about the courage to be honest, the bravery to feel, and the strength to connect. It's about finding your people, finding your path, and finding your way back to yourself. You don't have to summit Everest to heal; you don't need a passport or weeks off work to begin. You just need the willingness to take the first step. To say yes to the wildness within you and around you. To say yes to a new kind of strength.

If you're ready to step out of the fog and onto the trail, I'll be walking it with you.

Let's roll.

Chapter 1: Cracks in the Armor

I was always a sensitive kid, though you probably wouldn't have known it from the outside, or so I hoped. Like many boys, I learned early and instinctively to keep the most vulnerable parts of myself hidden. My feelings, my thoughts, my fears, they became a secret language spoken only in the quiet, lonely corners of my mind. Beneath the surface of everything I did, there was a constant, quiet hum, a low-frequency broadcast that played on an endless loop with a single, devastating message: you're not good enough.

For years, I couldn't put a name to it; I simply knew, with a certainty that felt as real and unchangeable as the ground beneath my feet, that I would never quite measure up. This deep-seated conviction of unworthiness was a heavy, invisible weight I carried with me everywhere, into classrooms, onto sports fields, and into my own home. It was a persistent whisper that followed me, telling me I was inherently flawed, that no matter what I did, it simply wouldn't be enough. This is a feeling so many men know, a quiet soundtrack of inadequacy that plays under even our biggest and most celebrated achievements, a private knowledge that we are always just one mistake away from being exposed as impostors.

Psychologists call this feeling of being a fraud "imposter syndrome," but that clinical term doesn't quite capture the raw, gut-level reality of it. It's not just a thought; it's a full-body experience. It's the tightening in your chest when you're asked for your opinion in a meeting, the slick of sweat on your palms before a presentation, the compulsive need to replay a conversation in your head, searching for the misstep that will surely lead to your unmasking.

It's the sharp, metallic taste of fear during a varsity possession drill, my lungs burning as I tried to keep up with guys who were two or three years older and already young men. As one of the only freshmen on the team, I felt like an imposter in a stolen jersey, my every touch on the ball a frantic audition to prove I belonged. The speed was blistering, a chaotic blur of bigger, stronger bodies. When the coach's whistle sliced through the air, I was just grateful for the chance to stop moving. He was yelling about our shape, about the lazy passes that were killing our momentum, but I was lost in my own private terror. The hum was deafening, a constant broadcast reminding me I was the kid, the weak link, the one they were all waiting to see fail. When his eyes locked onto mine and he asked the whole group, "Who can tell me why we're getting sliced through the middle every time?" my blood ran cold. I saw it instantly: one of the senior defenders, a guy I revered, was pushing up too far, leaving a huge gap behind him. But the thought of saying that out loud, of calling out a senior, felt like a sin I couldn't commit.

My mind raced with the unwritten rules of the team hierarchy. You're a freshman. You don't correct seniors. Ever. The internal critic was screaming: Keep your mouth shut. They'll think you're arrogant. You'll be on the bench for the rest of the season. I could feel the captain's stare on me, a silent challenge. I desperately avoided eye contact, focusing on a patch of chewed-up turf as if it held the secrets of the universe. A moment later, the captain spoke, his voice dripping with the easy authority I envied. "Jimmy's getting pulled out of position, Coach. It leaves the back line exposed." The coach nodded, and the senior defender shot the captain a look of respect. There was no argument. And in that instant, I was flooded with profound and suffocating shame. It wasn't just that I had been silent; it was that I had been a coward. I had proven to myself and everyone else that I was just a kid at the men's table, afraid to even speak.

For boys, this often begins when we first realize there's a script for masculinity that we don't know how to read.

I remember one specific moment with perfect clarity. I was maybe twelve, sitting in the pungent, humid air of a middle school locker room after a soccer game we'd lost badly. I was already feeling the sting of the loss, the burn of my own clumsy mistakes on the field. The older boys, the eighth graders, were talking. Their voices were loud, confident, full of a casual bravado I couldn't comprehend. They joked about the game, about girls, about weekend plans. I sat on the bench, pretending to be busy with the laces on my cleats, my head down. I wanted to join in, to say something witty or cool, but my throat felt tight, and my mind was blank. All I could think was, don't say something stupid. Just be invisible.

One of the popular kids, a forward, looked over at me. "Yadon, you were quiet out there today. Cat got your tongue?"

A few guys snickered and said something I couldn't hear. My face flushed hot with shame. I mumbled something like, "Nah, just tired," my voice barely a squeak. I couldn't meet his eyes. In that moment, the hum grew louder. It was a low thrum behind my ears, a vibration of pure inadequacy. It was the screamingly loud internal message: See? You don't belong here. You're different. You're weak. That feeling of being on the outside, of being fundamentally different from the guys who seemed to have the rulebook for being a man memorized, became a cornerstone of my identity. I learned that safety was in silence. I learned that the best way to hide my sensitivity was to build a wall around it, brick by painstaking brick.

By sophomore year, the hum wasn't just in my head; it had taken up residence in my body. I'd sit in class, the math teacher scribbling formulas on the board, and I would feel this tightness in my chest, like I'd swallowed a fist. The smallest mistakes, a wrong answer, a stumble in the hallway, were like flares to a critic I couldn't see but could feel breathing down my neck. At home, I'd retreat to my room and close the door, not because I wanted privacy, but because it was the only space where I could finally exhale without wondering who was watching. It wasn't depression as I understood it back then. It was more like carrying an invisible rucksack everywhere, one that nobody else seemed to notice, but I couldn't take it off, no matter how much I wanted to.

That hum grew louder as I hit my teenage years, swelling from a subtle, almost imperceptible thrum to a roaring, chaotic noise in my head. The volume was always loudest when I was comparing myself to others: the star athletes, the popular kids with easy smiles, the ones whose parents weren't constantly stressed and arguing about money. I would watch them moving through the crowded school hallways with a casual grace, laughing and untroubled, and the hum inside me would swell into a scream, "See? You're not like them. You'll never be like them." Any criticism, whether it was real or just something I had imagined, would land like a physical blow, especially if it touched on my intelligence or my ability to be "manly." If a coach yelled at me for not being tough enough, or a teacher implied I wasn't smart enough, it was like gasoline on the fire, a loud and clear confirmation of the deepest fears I held about myself.

Then, at seventeen, my already fragile world tilted on its axis and broke apart. My girlfriend got pregnant.

The moment she told me is frozen in time. We were sitting in our graphic design class after she came in late from a doctor's appointment. She was crying, her words catching in her throat as she showed me the positive pregnancy test.

I remember the plastic stick felt impossibly small and light in my hand, but it carried the weight of a collapsing universe. I didn't feel joy or excitement. I felt a cold, terrifying dread wash over me, a wave of panic so intense it felt like I was drowning. My carefully constructed facade, the one that was already cracking under the strain of adolescence, completely crumbled. The roaring hum in my head became deafening.

Telling my parents was one of the hardest things I've ever had to do. I made my mom drive us an hour into the city to meet my older sister to help me tell them. I had already called her on the phone, freaking out. I saw the shock on my mom's face, the way her hand flew to her mouth. I saw the look on my dad's face, not anger, but a deep, weary disappointment that was a thousand times worse. His silence was an indictment, but I was lucky enough that, despite the disappointment, my parents were supportive from that moment. The conversation with her parents was a full-blown inferno of rage and accusations. I sat on their couch, a seventeen-year-old boy, and listened as they detailed all the ways I had ruined their daughter's life and how she should get rid of the baby. They weren't wrong to be mad, but wrong to suggest that their daughter get rid of the baby.

In the surreal and terrifying span of a few months between my junior and senior year of high school, we were married in a small, tense ceremony at my aunt's small church. I dropped out of high school, earned a GED, and went from being a kid worried about classes and grades to being a husband and a father.

Let me be clear: I loved my daughter from the very second I found out she was going to exist. That love was the only clear, solid thing in a world that had become a violent storm of shame and judgment. But love wasn't enough to silence the noise. In the eyes of the world, I was no longer a student with potential; I was a cautionary tale. I felt the whispers and averted glances in the hallways of the school. My teachers, who had once encouraged me, now looked at me with a kind of pity that felt like contempt. My self-worth, which had been fragile to begin with, shattered into a million pieces.

I was just a boy, crushed by the suffocating, iron-heavy weight of adult expectations: to provide, to protect, to have it all figured out when, in reality, I felt utterly and completely lost. I remember the white-knuckled panic of trying to magically conjure money out of thin air when I was working a minimum-wage job at a gas station. I was supposed to be the strong one, the protector, but I couldn't even protect myself from the storm that was raging inside my own head.

My response was a desperate, panicked retreat from a reality that felt too painful to face. I gained sixty pounds while my wife was pregnant, eating my fear and shame in late-night runs to fast-food joints. My days became a blur of avoidance: sleeping in late, staying up all night, and losing myself for hours upon hours in the digital worlds of video games. The controller in my hand was a shield, the screen a portal to a place where I could be a hero, where I could succeed, where the crushing weight of my life couldn't follow me. It was a conscious attempt to escape the relentless noise in my head, to numb the shame and the fear that were my constant companions.

Even as I tried to be a loving dad, holding my daughter, playing with her, caring for her the best I could, a significant part of me was always absent, lost in the thick fog of my inadequacy. The disconnect was agonizing. I was there physically, but emotionally, I was a ghost. I wasn't a great husband. I wasn't mean or cruel; I was simply… absent. Emotionally vacant. Drowning in my head. My mind was always a million miles away, consumed by the anxieties and that damn internal hum that I didn't know how to silence. I suppressed everything like fear, frustration, shame, and sadness, because I had been taught, and had come to believe, that to show those emotions would only be a final confirmation of my weakness.

Every once in a while, though, the fog would lift. I remember one night my daughter, barely a toddler, was on the floor with a stuffed animal that made a ridiculous squeak when you squeezed it. She kept handing it to me, grinning every time I made it squeal. Ten minutes later, I realized I hadn't thought about bills, failure, or the future once. She had pulled me into her world without even trying. It made me wonder how many of those moments I'd already missed because I was buried in my head.

This experience, while deeply personal, is not unique. Researchers have found that young fathers, particularly those navigating unplanned pregnancies, experience heightened levels of anxiety, depression, and identity confusion. A 2017 study found that young dads were more likely than their peers to feel isolated, judged, and unsupported, and, like me, most of them never reached out for help; many didn't even know they could. This is compounded by the general stressors of parenthood, which a 2023 advisory from the U.S. Surgeon General noted can leave nearly half of all parents feeling completely overwhelmed on most days. For a young man already predisposed to feelings of inadequacy, this pressure cooker of financial strain and societal judgment becomes a full-blown crisis of identity.

When that marriage inevitably ended a few years later, I was already buried under the belief that I had failed. That I was a failure. This belief, as a 2021 American Psychological Association survey found, is a common scar for men who internalize early "failures" not as setbacks, but as a permanent and damning indictment of their worth. That was me. That sense of failure shaped everything that came next. I threw myself into a frantic pursuit of achievement, a desperate attempt to outrun the ghost of my past.

I went to EMT school, driven by a need to prove I could be a savior, a competent man in a crisis. I started working in EMS, then earned a bachelor's in Exercise Science and began teaching. But the hum was still there, so I immediately pursued a master's degree, then an Education Specialist Degree, just one step below a doctorate. Each degree, each certification, was another brick in a new wall I was building, a wall of accomplishments designed to hide the scared kid still cowering inside. Eventually, in a strange twist of fate, I found myself working at the very high school I had quit almost twenty years before.

By any external measure, this was success. I had proven them all wrong. I was the cautionary tale who had rewritten his own ending. But deep down, the hum was still there. That little voice telling me, "It's not enough." I had come to realize that no one in this world, outside of my family, truly cared for what I had accomplished. I hadn't proven anything to anyone else, so why was it so hard to prove it to myself?

This deep-seated feeling of inadequacy is a cornerstone of the poor mental health that plagues so many men. We carry this invisible weight, assuming it's normal, believing that every other man has it figured out, and if we don't, we're the ones who're broken. This is how depression so often manifests in men, not always as sadness, but as irritability, anger, escapism, or the relentless pursuit of achievement. What society often rewards as "strength", like stoicism, emotional control, and relentless self-reliance, are frequently the very symptoms of our underlying distress and the barriers that prevent us from seeking help. The armor we build to appear strong becomes a prison.

Let me be clear: traits like self-reliance, discipline, and courage are foundational. I even believe in stoicism to a degree, but we should be working to improve these traits on our journey. But it must be done in a way that is emotionally healthy and sustainable. It would take me years to begin untangling these knots. I'm still working on it today. But that period of my life, that trial by fire, was the first real crack in my armor. It was the first time I began to realize that the traditional expectations of manhood in today's society weren't just hard... they were silent killers. And that maybe, just maybe, my sensitivity wasn't a weakness after all. Perhaps it was a warning sign, a flare lighting up a deep wound I hadn't yet learned how to treat.

This chapter of my life didn't end in a glorious redemption. There was no perfect comeback. There was just a long, bruised road ahead, and the first few fumbling steps forward. If you're in that place right now, walking through a fog of your own, just know this: you are not the only one. And feeling broken doesn't mean you are.

Actionable Insights for the Trail Ahead

- **Name the Hum**. That constant, quiet voice of "you're not good enough" isn't just background noise; it's a signal. To diminish its power, you must first identify its message. Take ten minutes this week with a notebook. At the top of the page, write, "What is the Hum telling me today?" Don't censor yourself. Let the critic have its say on paper. Is it about your job? Your role as a father? A mistake you made yesterday? Then, for each accusation, ask yourself, "Whose voice does this sound like?" Often, you'll find it's the echo of a parent, a coach, or a past failure. Seeing its accusations in black and white is the first step to robbing them of their power.

- **Reflect on Your Armor.** Think about the early pressures from family, friends, or society that shaped your definition of "strength". Take out another sheet of paper and create two columns. In the first column, list 3-5 unwritten "rules of manhood" you learned as a boy (e.g., "Men don't ask for help," "Never let them see you cry," "Your worth is what you earn"). In the second column, write one specific example of how that rule has either helped you or hurt you in your adult life. This isn't about blame; it's about taking inventory of the beliefs that might now be contributing to your isolation or emotional absence.

- **Journal Your Unspoken**. Even if it feels uncomfortable or "unmanly," get a notebook and commit to a five-minute "brain dump" three times this week. The prompt is simple: "What I'm really feeling is...". Don't try to be profound or even coherent. Just write whatever comes to mind without judgment, anger, fear, frustration, or resentment. The simple act of translating internal chaos into words on a page creates a small crack in the armor, a vital step toward recognizing the wound that needs treatment.

- **Seek Shared Stories.** You are not alone in these struggles. This week, find one podcast, book, or online forum where men are openly discussing their experiences with inadequacy or shame. As you listen or read, pay attention to the feeling of recognition in your own body. Hearing another man describe a feeling you thought was yours alone is a powerful antidote to isolation. It validates your feelings and serves as a crucial reminder that this is a shared human experience, not a personal failing.

- **Redefine Success for Yourself**. If you find yourself on the hamster wheel of constantly striving to prove your worth, take 30 minutes to define what success truly means to you, independent of anyone else's opinion. Break your life into four categories: My Role as a Partner, My Role as a father, My Professional Life, and My Relationship with Myself. For each category, write one sentence that defines a successful outcome that has nothing to do with money, status, or external validation. This new definition is your compass. Put it somewhere you can see it regularly.

Discussion Questions

- The author describes a "constant, quiet hum of 'you're not good enough'". Can you identify a similar internal "hum" or critical voice in your own life? What specific messages or experiences contributed to its development?

- How did societal expectations of manhood (e.g., "provide, protect, figure it out") impact the author as a young father? How have these or similar expectations affected you during challenging life transitions?

- The author discusses emotional vacancy and suppressing feelings. What emotions do you find most challenging to express, and what fears or beliefs prevent you from doing so?

- The chapter highlights that men often express depression differently (irritability, anger, escapism). Have you or men you know experienced these "masked" forms of distress? How might this affect diagnosis and help-seeking?

Chapter 2: Trauma in the Rearview

The thing I have learned about trauma is that it doesn't always announce itself loudly. It doesn't always scream for attention. Sometimes it just lingers quietly, patient, heavy. It's like a fog that rolls into a valley so slowly you don't notice it until you're surrounded, a fog that subtly changes the landscape of your mind, muting the colors, muffling the sounds, and making everything a little harder to navigate. It simply settles into the background of your life, becoming a new, oppressive normal you barely notice until the day you realize you're suffocating in plain sight.

My early years in Emergency Medical Services were not overtly traumatic in the way you see in movies, no daily explosions or dramatic, life-saving surgeries in the field. They were a different kind of draining, a slow burn of the soul. I started out doing non-emergency transport jobs, endless, repetitive runs from nursing homes to doctors' appointments and back again. While the work honed my technical skills, I could start an IV in a moving vehicle on a bumpy road without thinking; it was a slow erosion of purpose.

I remember one patient, an elderly woman. We transported her three times a week for dialysis. She was ninety-three, with skin like wrinkled parchment and eyes that held a universe of stories she rarely told. Her room at the nursing home smelled faintly of lavender, antiseptic, and soiled linens. Every Monday, Wednesday, and Friday, we'd find her sitting in her wheelchair by the window, a small, worn photo album on her lap. During the rides, she was mostly silent, but sometimes she would open the album and talk about her late husband, or the sprawling garden she used to keep. "Her husband planted those roses the day our son was born," she'd say, her finger tracing the faded edge of a photograph. "You should have seen them in June."

The trauma wasn't in the medical procedure; it was in the quiet, profound loneliness that filled the back of that ambulance. It was in the realization that for three hours a week, my partner and I were her only consistent human contact. Each drop-off back at the silent, sterile nursing home felt like a small death, a fresh abandonment. We'd wheel her back to her room, help her into her chair by the window, and she would just say, "See you Wednesday, boys." The door would click shut behind us, leaving her alone with the ghosts in her photo album. A single run like that is just a sad day at work. But hundreds of them, stacked one on top of the other, begin to form a weight. It was a burnout born not from chaos, but from a profound and grinding lack of meaning, a constant, low-grade exposure to the quiet suffering of the world.

That all changed when I moved into 911 work. That's when the black cloud showed up. In EMS, we all joked about the cloud. It was a grim superstition, a metaphor for the inexplicable runs of bad luck and horrific calls that seemed to follow certain people. Some medics, the lucky ones, seemed to avoid their entire careers, running routine calls and never having to face the true abyss. Others, like me, got picked. Not because I was reckless or chasing adrenaline, but just... because. It felt like a grim lottery no one wanted to win, a dark badge of honor for those who were destined to see too much and did not know how to process it.

People enter public service with a deep-seated desire to help; you have to be driven by it, or you won't last. Like many misguided rookies, I went in with a hero complex, my head filled with visions from television shows where we saved lives in every episode. The reality of the job is a much harder, colder lesson. I learned, call by agonizing call, that you can't save them all. That is a tough pill to swallow, a pill that, even a decade off the ambulance and in the relative (or so I thought) safety of a classroom, I believe is still stuck going down. It is the searing, humbling realization that sometimes, even when you do everything perfectly, by the book, it still isn't enough.

You never, ever forget the pediatric calls either. The ones that don't make it. The ones where you find yourself doing CPR on a child who looks like your own kid, your hands working on a tiny, fragile chest while your own heart is breaking into a million pieces.

I remember the moment the call came over the radio. The dispatcher's voice was tense, stripped of its usual calm cadence. "Medic 607, respond to a one-year-old male, unresponsive, not breathing." A chill went through the cab of the ambulance. Pediatric cardiac arrest. The two words every EMT dreads. The drive to the scene was a blur of adrenaline and focus. My partner was a veteran who rarely showed emotion, but I could see the tightness in his jaw as he navigated traffic, the siren screaming. We didn't speak. We were both running through the protocols in our heads, calculating drug dosages for a tiny body, mentally preparing for the scene we knew was waiting for us.

We burst through the door of the small single-wide trailer, and the world went into slow motion. A half-eaten bowl of cereal was on the coffee table; a bright blue dinosaur toy lay on its side by the couch. The silence in the room was deafening, broken only by the mother's choked, rhythmic sobs. She was on the phone with the 911 dispatcher, her face a mask of disbelief and horror. The father stood frozen in the corner, his back against the wall, his eyes wide and vacant.

Our focus was on the small, still form on the floor. My training took over. I was a machine performing a function, my mind detached, my hands moving with a precision born of endless drills. Check for a pulse. Start compressions. Get the airway open. My partner was setting up the pediatric bag, his movements economical and swift. But my eyes saw the things the training doesn't prepare you for. The small, faded teddy bear in the crib in the next room. The impossibly tiny sneakers by the door. The smell of baby powder hanging in the air.

We worked on him for what felt like an eternity, the small, rhythmic thud of my compressions, the only sound other than the mother's weeping. But there was nothing. No response. When we finally called it, when the moment came to stop, the silence that followed was the most profound I have ever experienced. It was the sound of a universe ending.

Later, back in the ambulance, the silence was different. It was heavy, thick with everything we couldn't say. My partner just stared out the windshield as I drove. We didn't talk about it. We never did. That was the rule. Back at the station, we went through the motions. We cleaned the rig with a disinfectant that couldn't wash away the smell of the trailer. We restocked the cabinets, replacing the tiny IV catheters and breathing tubes we had used. We completed the paperwork, reducing the immense tragedy to a series of checkboxes and sterile medical terms. My partner finally broke the silence. "Tough one," he grunted, before disappearing into the break room. That was it. That was all the processing we were allowed.

But the image of that blue dinosaur never left me. It would appear in my mind at random moments in the middle of the night, while I was driving, while I was playing with my daughter. Those images, those sounds, those smells are seared into my memory with the permanence of a cattle brand. These weren't just scenes I witnessed; they were visceral experiences that became a part of me, lingering long after the sirens faded, replaying in my mind, and leaving a cold, hollow ache in my chest that never fully went away.

People think the hard part is the call itself. It's not. It's the way it sneaks back into your head while you're brushing your teeth or trying to fall asleep. Trauma doesn't live in the moment; it lives in the rewinds.

The calls without clear endings were often the hardest. Not just the ones we lost, but the ones where we had to make impossible choices under pressure, decisions that felt less like medicine and more like a grim, hurried calculation of suffering.

We were dispatched to a multi-car pileup on a dark, slick stretch of highway one night. The scene was a tangle of twisted metal and shattered glass, illuminated by the chaotic strobing of emergency lights. The air was thick with the smell of coolant and something metallic that I would later recognize as the smell of blood. My partner and I were the first medics on scene, and we immediately began the rapid, systematic process of assessing the injured. There were multiple victims, all of them scared, hurt, and calling for help. Our training was to quickly sort out the injured to determine who needed immediate life-saving care versus who could wait.

I moved from one car to the next, my mind a checklist of protocols. That's when I came to a minivan, its front end crushed. In the driver's seat, a man was unconscious, pinned by the steering wheel, his breathing shallow and labored. He was my priority. As I worked to get an airway established and assess the extent of his internal injuries, a woman in the passenger seat of the car next to his started screaming for me.

"Please, you have to help my husband!" she cried. Her face was bleeding from a cut on her forehead, but her eyes were fixed on the driver of her car. He was conscious, moaning in pain from what looked like a broken arm. He was hurt badly, but he was breathing. He was stable for the moment.

"Ma'am, I will be there as soon as I can," I told her, my voice strained, my focus entirely on the silent man in front of me who was minutes away from dying.

"No, now! Please! He's in so much pain!" she begged, her voice raw with terror and desperation. Every instinct in my body, every fiber of my being that had pushed me into this line of work, wanted to go to her, to comfort her, to treat her husband's obvious and agonizing pain. But I couldn't. The man in the minivan was silently slipping away. To leave him would have been a death sentence. And so, I had to tune her out. I had to treat her desperate pleas as background noise while I continued to work on the unresponsive stranger in front of me.

We eventually got the man out of the minivan and into an ambulance. Other units arrived and took care of the woman and her husband. But her voice stayed with me. The moral weight of that decision, having to ignore one person's suffering to treat another's, was something they don't prepare you for in training. It's not a medical failure, but it feels like a human one. I made the right call according to every protocol in the book, but for weeks afterward, her voice would echo in my head as I tried to fall asleep. The man I helped died a few days later. That incident added a new layer to the trauma I was accumulating, not just the trauma of what I saw, but the burden of the choices I was forced to make.

The calls kept coming, each one adding another thin layer of sediment to the growing weight in my soul. I wasn't just accumulating memories; my body's chemistry was changing. In training, they teach you about the adrenal system, the miraculous surge of fight-or-flight hormones that allow you to lift a heavy patient or stay calm in the face of chaos. It's designed for short, acute bursts. What they don't prepare you for is a life lived in a perpetual state of low-grade activation. My adrenal system, designed for emergencies, was now constantly simmering. My body was marinating in a bath of cortisol and stress hormones; my amygdala, which is the brain's alarm system, was stuck in the 'on' position. I was hypervigilant, scanning for threats everywhere, even at home.

I remember one night, my daughter, then a toddler, woke up crying from a bad dream. I went into her room, and as I picked her up to comfort her, I felt my heart pounding, my senses on high alert, my eyes scanning the dark corners of her room for an intruder. My body couldn't distinguish between a child's nightmare and a 3 a.m. dispatch call. I was a first responder in my own home, and the people I loved most were getting the hypervigilant, emotionally numb shell of a man who was leaving his real self behind in the back of an ambulance.

The first time I taught a CPR class as a teacher, a year after I officially left the ambulance, the training video showed an infant resuscitation scene. A wave of nausea and panic hit me so hard I had to physically turn and walk out of the room. I stood in the empty hallway, my heart pounding, my hands shaking, trying to catch my breath like the ghost of that little boy in the trailer with the blue dinosaur toy filling the space around me. No one knew why I'd left. How do you explain that to a room full of teenagers? How do you say, "I just relived one of the worst moments of my life in a simulation and now I can't breathe"? You don't. You swallow it down, you pretend you're fine, you splash some cold water on your face, and you hope no one asks. You just keep going.

That's what I did for years. Shift after grueling shift. Twenty-four hours on, then another thirteen in a different county. No rest. No sleep. Just a toxic cocktail of caffeine, adrenaline, chaos, and a deep, simmering self-hatred for not being stronger. I wasn't living; I was surviving. My body became a machine, but my mind was a battlefield. The black cloud was no longer a metaphor; it was a constant, low-grade sensation of dread that had settled over my entire life.

I remember mentioning to a paramedic partner one shift that I was struggling. We were sitting in the ambulance, the stale air thick with the smell of old coffee and disinfectants. I kept it vague, just a comment about feeling burned out. He was one of those guys who worked constantly, never home, a leader in another department in the next county over. I'll never forget his response. He didn't even look at me. He just stared out the windshield and said, "Get over it. We all deal with it." That was it. In that moment, the small flicker of courage it took for me to speak up was extinguished. The message was clear: your pain is not unique, and it is certainly not welcome. I felt worthless, ashamed for even trying. I think about that moment sometimes and wonder if he's still carrying the same weight just quieter. I wonder if I missed a chance to show him there was another way. But back then, I didn't have another way to offer. I barely had one for myself.

My breaking point wasn't a call. It was a quiet moment in my own house, alone. The black cloud had soaked through everything in my life, and I couldn't see a way out. The hours leading up to that moment were a torrent of despair. Images from calls flashed through my mind like a broken film projector. I saw the blue dinosaur. I saw the woman from the car accident. I heard the frantic voices of dispatchers. Overlaid on it all was the relentless screaming of my own failure: as a husband, a father, a man. Everyone would be better off without me. I'm a burden. I can't fix this. This pain will never end. I came within a single second of pulling the trigger. In that critical, final second, a single, vivid image flashed through my mind: my daughter's face, her innocent smile. It was just enough. It was the crack of light that pulled me back from the brink.

It wasn't just a smiling face; it was a full memory that crashed through the suffocating gray fog in my mind. It was from years earlier. I was sitting on the living room floor, numb, staring at nothing, and my daughter, who was four at the time, padded over to me. She didn't say anything. She just leaned her small, warm body against my side and slipped her hand into mine. I can still feel the impossible smallness of her fingers, the complete and unquestioning trust in that simple gesture. In my mind's eye, in that final second, I saw her looking up at me, her brow furrowed with a seriousness that only a child can have, and she had asked, "Daddy, are you sad?"

That memory, that feeling of her hand in mine, became an anchor in the storm of my self-hatred. It wasn't a thought of happiness that saved me; it was a question of responsibility that was so profound it was paralyzing. Who will hold this hand tomorrow? Who will walk her to her first day of school? Who will be there to see the woman she becomes? The image of her growing up in a world where her father was a ghost, a cautionary tale, a man who gave up, it was a pain that was, for the first time, sharper than the pain I was trying to escape. The cold, heavy weight in my hand suddenly felt obscene. The decision to end things had felt like a final, merciful surrender, but the memory of her small hand transformed it into an act of profound and unforgivable abandonment. A sob I hadn't realized was caught in my throat finally broke free, a raw, ragged sound that filled the silence of the room.

Instead of ending my life, I chose to try and save it. I chose therapy. It was a terrifying step. I was ashamed, scared of what it would mean to admit I needed help, of being seen as weak or broken by a world that had taught me real men handle it alone. That internal resistance, the voice of my conditioning, screamed at me. But my desperation finally outweighed the shame.

I remember the first session. I sat in a generic waiting room with bland art on the walls, my leg bouncing uncontrollably. Every instinct told me to run. When the therapist called my name, I felt like a defendant being called to the stand. I sat on his couch, my arms crossed tightly over my chest. He was a kind-looking man with gentle eyes. He asked me a simple question: "So, what brings you in today?" I couldn't speak. My throat was a knot of unshed tears and unspoken pain. After a long, heavy silence, I finally managed to whisper, "I don't think I can do this anymore." The moment those words left my mouth, something inside me broke. It was a mix of sheer terror and the most profound relief I had ever felt. For two months that summer, I lifted weights and sat on that couch, unpacking emotions I didn't even know I was carrying. The most surprising discovery was the immense, white-hot anger I had buried for the world, but mostly at myself for feeling weak. The most difficult part was admitting, out loud, how deeply I believed I was a failure, and I will admit I struggle with this at times, even now as I write this book.

This personal crisis was a symptom of a systemic one. The mental health toll on EMTs is alarmingly high. Studies show that EMS professionals experience PTSD, depression, and anxiety at rates significantly higher than the general population. This phenomenon is often the result of what researchers call "compassion fatigue" or "secondary traumatic stress." Unlike burnout, which is a gradual erosion from overwork, compassion fatigue is a more acute response to the constant exposure to the suffering of others. The American Institute of Stress describes it as a state where caregivers begin to mirror the symptoms of the trauma victims they are trying to help. Our emotional detachment was a survival tool on the job, but it was corrosive to our lives back home. Tragically, EMTs are 1.39 times more likely to die by suicide. In one study, male EMTs reported feeling socially isolated within their trauma, afraid to speak up for fear of being seen as weak. But that's not healing. That's just hiding.

I didn't heal back then. I hid. I buried the trauma and went back to school, becoming a teacher. Years later, a school shooting unburied it all for me. I had to step out of my classroom to make copies when the lockdown alert sounded. As I ran back toward my classroom, I heard the shots, sharp, unmistakable cracks echoing through the atrium. My EMS training kicked in, a cold, detached assessment of chaos. My instincts, honed by years on the ambulance, screamed at me to run toward the sound, to find my students, to protect them, to act. My mind scanning for the closest AED and trauma kit with the sole purpose of helping anyone injured because I am the only one in the building who could. But someone pulled me into a closet in the media center. I stayed hidden, my body trembling with adrenaline and a suppressed, helpless rage.

This helplessness was different. As an EMT, helplessness was a battle against the limits of medicine. This was the helplessness of a protector unable to protect, a leader forced into hiding while his kids were in danger. Let me be clear, I have no deep vision of taking on a bad guy and taking the fight to the shooter. I am not dumb. But I know my ability to help, and I could have. It was a profound violation of my sense of purpose, a direct assault on my core identity as a man. It wrecked me.

That night, I didn't sleep. My wife asked me what was wrong, and I told her I was fine, three of the most dishonest words in the English language. In reality, every time I closed my eyes, I saw the atrium in slow motion, the sunlight slanting across the tile, and the sharp *pop-pop-pop* echoing off the walls and the SRO's shouting commands. My brain kept trying to rewrite the scene, imagining myself getting there in time, doing something, anything to provide care for those who needed it, but every version ended the same way: me standing there, frozen, my hands empty. I'd never felt so much like a bystander in my own life.

In the week that followed, the world felt surreal. There were vigils and memorials. Counselors were brought into the school, but I avoided them. I told myself others needed it more. But the deeper, more honest truth is, I didn't think I mattered enough to take a spot, and I still don't want to take away that resource from my colleagues and students.

The true cost of the event revealed itself at home. My fuse was nonexistent. One night, my son spilled a glass of milk at the dinner table, and I erupted with a terrifyingly disproportionate rage. He burst into tears, and my wife looked at me with a mixture of fear and confusion. I didn't have the words to explain that the spilled milk felt like another loss of control in a world that had just been shattered. The re-traumatization was not just an internal experience; it was a poison seeping into the lives of the people I loved most.

When summer came and the constant noise of the school year quieted, everything hit me. Hard. The pain I'd buried a decade before came roaring back, now intertwined with this new trauma. So, I did what I always did: I tried to outrun it. I wrote books, built a website, and started a business that cost me money and made none. It was busy work and therapy wrapped into one. The fog that had started in the back of an ambulance had rolled in again, thicker than ever. And I still didn't know how to fully walk out of it.

Research confirms that survivors of school shootings, including staff, suffer from long-term traumatic stress and a shattered sense of safety. For me, already carrying unaddressed trauma, the shooting re-traumatized me, overwhelming the coping mechanisms I had so carefully constructed. My armor had failed. Recovery, I was learning, isn't just about processing an event; it's about the long, arduous journey of rebuilding a shattered sense of trust in the world and in yourself.

If you've lived through trauma, especially if you've buried it like I did, know this: it doesn't disappear just because you pretend it's not there. And your silence doesn't make you stronger. It just makes you lonelier. There is another way forward. It's slower. It's harder. It asks you to feel things you'd rather not. But it also heals.

Actionable Insights for the Trail Ahead

- **Acknowledge the Lingering.** Trauma doesn't vanish; it leaves a "black cloud" that can affect your sleep, mood, and relationships. This week, practice acknowledging its presence without judgment. When a wave of anxiety, a flash of anger, or a feeling of numbness arises, simply say to yourself, "This is the trauma talking. It's an echo of the past, not a predictor of the future." Pay attention to hidden physical signs like chronic headaches or digestive issues, as these can be manifestations of unaddressed trauma. This isn't about dwelling on the past, but about honoring the reality of your experience so you can begin to separate from it.

- **Challenge the "Tough-It-Out" Mentality.** Many male-dominated cultures reinforce the idea that you should "man up". This chapter is a testament to the ultimate failure of that approach. This week, identify one area of your life where you are "toughing it out" at great personal cost. Then, write down the honest answer to this question: "What is the real cost of my silence in this area?" Is it your connection with your wife? Your patience with your kids? Your physical health? Seeing the cost in black and white makes the need for a new strategy undeniable.

- **Identify Your "Black Cloud."** What are the specific ways that unaddressed stress and trauma manifest in your life? Is it through irritability with your family? A pattern of withdrawing from your friends? Escapism into work, alcohol, or hobbies? Physical symptoms that have no clear cause? Naming these specific manifestations is the first step toward understanding them. Journal about when these feelings arise and how they impact your daily life, not to judge them, but simply to gather data on how your trauma is speaking to you.

- **Frame Therapy as a "Crack of Light."** If you're considering therapy, it's crucial to reframe what it means. It is not an admission of being broken. View it as a strategic and powerful step towards understanding your internal landscape and finding a path forward. Address the common fear of "what will I even say?" by preparing for your first session. Write down the top three things that are causing you pain right now. That's your starting point. The therapist's job is to guide the conversation from there.

- **Be the First to Speak.** If you're in a position of influence, a father, manager, coach, or friend, consider sharing your own experiences with seeking help when appropriate. You don't need to share intimate details. A simple, low-stakes statement can be revolutionary. For example: "I was feeling burned out last year, and I started talking to a professional about it. It's been incredibly helpful for me to have that space." Normalizing conversation is the most crucial step in breaking down the stigma for others. Your courage can create a ripple effect that, quite literally, could save a life.

Discussion Questions

- The author describes trauma as a "black cloud" that lingers. How has unaddressed trauma or chronic stress manifested in your own life (e.g., in your sleep, appetite, relationships, or level of irritability)?

- The "tough-it-out" culture is highlighted as a major barrier in male-dominated professions. In what areas of your life or work have you felt pressure to suppress emotions or "just keep going" despite internal struggle? What were the consequences?

- The author's decision to seek therapy, despite shame and fear, was a "crack of light." What are your own perceptions of therapy? What barriers (internal or external) might prevent you or other men you know from seeking professional help?

- The author experienced a profound sense of helplessness during the school shooting. Can you recall a time when you felt similarly helpless, and how you coped with that feeling?

Chapter 3: The Weight of Ghosts: A Man's Guide to Grief and Loss

We aren't taught how to grieve; we're taught how to manage logistics. When loss comes, men are often handed an unspoken job title: Chief Logistics Officer of Sorrow. We're expected to make the calls, handle the arrangements, be the rock for everyone else to lean on, and project an aura of quiet strength while everyone else is allowed to fall apart. We learn to swallow our pain because we believe our duty is to absorb the pain of others. This isn't a personal failing; it's a script handed down through generations, a core component of a traditional masculinity that prioritizes stoicism over emotional honesty.

But grief isn't an administrative task. It's a seismic event. It's not a storm that passes. It's a fundamental shift in the landscape of your life. With each loss, another landmark is erased from the map of your world. First one, then another, until you look up one day and realize you're a stranger in your past, holding a useless map to a world that no longer exists. This chapter is for the man standing in that empty field, wondering where to go. It's about the cumulative weight of ghosts and finding a way to carry them with honor, not just with silence.

The First Lesson: A Man in Full

My first lesson in the silent, stoic script of male grief came when I was fourteen. My Papaw was a big and strong old man, the kind of man who seemed forged from a different, tougher era. He wasn't just a figure of authority; he was a legend in my young eyes. A Marine tanker who fought in the frozen landscapes of Korea. The head of security for NASA during the giddy, triumphant days of the Space Race and the moon landing. He was the man who later oversaw the secrets of the Nevada test sites. He was a pillar of strength, a living piece of American history.

But to me, he was the grandfather who would call every single grandchild on their birthday, his booming voice filling the phone line as he sang "Happy Birthday." He was the steady presence at family gatherings, a mountain of safety and quiet integrity. His strength was a given, a law of nature.

That's why watching him get sick felt like watching a mountain slowly crumble. The liver disease, a cruel legacy from his time at the test sites, began to eat away at him. The legend became frail. Our world shifted. My dad, his son, became his primary caregiver, staying at his house during the week while I was at school. On the weekends, it was my turn. At fourteen years old, I wasn't just visiting my grandparents; I was reporting for duty. I learned how to help my grandmother, how to be a caregiver, how to navigate the quiet, tense atmosphere of a sickroom where a great man was fading.

I was right there with him when he died. I was in the room and watched him take his last breath. There is no training for that moment, no way to prepare for the profound silence that follows a life's final exhale. In the immediate aftermath, a new chaos erupted. My grandmother, untethered from the man she had anchored her life to, was adrift in a sea of frantic energy and overwhelming pain. She was trying to do a hundred things at once, her movements sharp with panic and sorrow.

And the script was handed to me. My role, I understood without a word being said, was to be her anchor. To be strong. I remember my own tears, hot and insistent, the raw grief of a boy who had just lost his hero. But my sorrow felt like a luxury I couldn't afford. My duty was to my grandmother. I pushed my feelings down, packed them away, and focused on her. In the haze of those first few days, amidst the phone calls and the visitors and the quiet, heavy arrangements, no one asked me how I was feeling. They saw a boy being strong for his grandmother, and they commended him for it. I performed my role correctly.

I had learned the first lesson: a man's grief is his own private business, to be managed in silence, secondary to his duty. This experience isn't unique. It's a textbook example of how restrictive masculine norms condition boys to suppress their emotions. The belief that a man must maintain a stoic exterior acts as a significant barrier, preventing men from seeking help or even acknowledging the depth of their own pain. I had learned, at a formative age, that my emotional needs were a liability in a crisis. That was the first stone in the pack.

The Unfairness: A Brotherhood of One

The second wound was a different kind of violence. Losing a grandparent, however painful, follows the natural order of things. Losing your best friend at nineteen is a tear in the fabric of the universe. It's a theft of a future you believed was guaranteed.

Aaron was my childhood best friend. Even after my family moved away in middle school, we maintained that effortless bond that only comes from a shared history of skinned knees and secret jokes. He was the goofiest kid you'd ever meet, a lanky, laughing force of nature who could find the absurdity in anything. But beneath the humor, he was such a good person, the kind of loyal, decent friend you just assume will always be there, a constant in the background of your life story. I had just seen him a month before the phone call.

I remember the day with sickening clarity. I was at home, and the phone rang. My Mamaw, who was living with us after Papaw passed, answered and then handed the receiver to me. "It's for you," she said.

The voice on the other end was Aaron's dad. He sounded hollowed out, distant. He had actually asked to speak to my dad, but in her own grief, my Mamaw had misheard him. He didn't realize he was talking to me, Aaron's best friend, when he said the words. He spoke in a flat, disbelieving monotone. "Aaron was killed last night. In a car accident."

The world didn't just go silent; it ceased to exist. There was a roaring in my ears, and the floor seemed to tilt beneath my feet. It was a purely physical shock, a full-body rejection of a reality that was too brutal to comprehend. I was in utter shock, completely and totally broken.

What followed was a profound and lonely ache. The unique cruelty of our situation was that after I moved, we didn't have a shared circle of friends anymore. There was no group to huddle with for comfort. There was no one to call and say, "Hey, remember that time Aaron..." The stories, the inside jokes, the shared history all lived only with me. I had to carry that grief alone.

His funeral felt surreal. I was a stranger among the people who populated his new life, a ghost from his past. I watched his high school friends grieve together, supporting each other, and I felt a profound sense of isolation. I had lost my brother, but I had to mourn him in silence, a brotherhood of one. This isolated grief is a dangerous side effect of the "friendship recession" facing so many men. While women regularly get emotional support from their friends, only 21% of men say they do the same. Without that vital network of support, a man is left to process a devastating loss in an echo chamber, which only amplifies the pain. The U.S. Surgeon General has warned that this level of loneliness and isolation is as detrimental to long-term health as smoking fifteen cigarettes a day. My grief over Aaron wasn't just an emotional burden; it was a health crisis I didn't even know I was having.

The Compounding Storm

Grief, I learned, is not a series of single weather events. It's a climate that grows progressively heavier, the pressure building until the air is too thick to breathe.

My Mamaw's passing a few years later was another fundamental shift. She was, without exaggeration, the sweetest and kindest angel to have ever walked this earth. After Papaw died, she became an even more central part of our lives, a source of gentle, unconditional love. Her home was a safe harbor. Her loss wasn't a shock like Aaron's; it was an erosion. It felt like the world had lost some of its fundamental goodness, its color. They truly don't make people like her anymore, and her absence left a void that felt quiet but immense.

Then the storm truly broke. A couple of years later, my mom died. It was sudden, a catastrophic failure of her heart while she was visiting my older sister for the weekend. We all knew she had health issues, but we thought she had more time. You always think you have more time.

The shock was immense, and it was compounded by a terrifying variable: my dad was already in the throes of his own battle with melanoma. My parents had moved in with my wife and me by then, our house becoming a multi-generational triage unit of love and fear. I looked at my dad, already weakened by his fight, now stripped of his partner of decades, and I honestly thought he would give up. I thought the grief would extinguish the last of his will to fight.

He didn't. But my role shifted again. I was no longer just a son. I was a caregiver, a source of strength, and the de facto man of my own house, all while trying to navigate the raw, gaping wound of my own mother's death. The pressure was suffocating. How do you grieve your mother when you're terrified of losing your father? How do you hold your own sorrow when you're trying to be a pillar for his? The answer is, you don't. You pack it down. You focus on the logistics. You become the Chief Logistics Officer of Sorrow once more, because it's easier than feeling the full, terrifying weight of your own pain. Unprocessed grief like this often festers, and for men, it frequently manifests not as sadness, but as irritability, anger, and social withdrawal, the classic symptoms of male depression. I was becoming a textbook case, a man so busy managing his family's sorrow that he was blind to the ways his own grief was poisoning him from the inside out. This experience of grief manifesting as anger and physical distress is not just a psychological quirk; it's a physiological reality. Groundbreaking research, including studies on what is often termed "complicated grief," shows that unresolved loss can keep the body in a prolonged state of high alert. Dr. M. Katherine Shear at Columbia University's Center for Complicated Grief has shown that the brain patterns in those with complicated grief often resemble those seen in Post-Traumatic Stress Disorder (PTSD), with the amygdala, the brain's threat detector remaining chronically overactive. This leads to a constant, low-grade bath of stress hormones like cortisol, which, over time, can contribute to systemic inflammation, cardiovascular strain, and a weakened immune system. The "poison" I felt wasn't just a metaphor; it was the tangible result of my body trying to carry a burden my mind hadn't been allowed to process.

Watching my dad in the years that followed was its own form of grief. I had to watch my hero, the man who was my first and most powerful model of strength, become someone so completely broken down physically, mentally, and emotionally. It is a profound and painful thing to watch your parent become your child, to see the fear and vulnerability in the eyes of the person you always looked to for safety.

When he finally passed away, the feeling was not one of pure sadness. It was messy. Of course, it was hard; a central pillar of my life was gone. But interwoven with the sorrow was a quiet, almost shameful sense of relief. I knew he wasn't hurting anymore. The long, grueling battle was over. That feeling of relief mixed with grief is a complex emotion that men are rarely given permission to feel. We're taught that grief should be clean, simple sadness. But it's often a messy, contradictory cocktail of feelings, and the guilt over feeling anything but pure sorrow just becomes another stone in the pack.

The Weight of Ghosts

In the years that followed, my aunt and two of my cousins also died. The losses were no longer individual events; they were a pattern. A relentless subtraction. The continued loss of family members cemented this deep, pervasive feeling of being lonely for a world that no longer exists.

This is the cumulative weight of ghosts. It's the feeling of having a map to a city whose streets and landmarks have been erased one by one. The house you grew up in is sold. The restaurant where you had your first date is gone. And the people who were the true landmarks, the ones who held the stories, the history, the very context of your life, they are gone, too. You are still standing there, holding the map, but you're lost because the world it depicted has vanished. You are lost to the world you once knew.

This weight shows up in my life today. It's in the quiet moments when a memory ambushes me. It's in the reluctance to get too close to new people, a subconscious fear of another goodbye. It's in the low-grade sadness that can settle on a perfectly good day for no apparent reason. It's the feeling that the team I started with is gone, and I'm one of the last players left on the field. The psychological toll of these multiple, unresolved losses is real; it's a form of complex trauma where the nervous system never gets a chance to return to baseline, leaving you in a perpetual state of low-grade alert and emotional exhaustion.

Actionable Insights for the Trail Ahead

- **Acknowledge the Script and Defy It.** The first step is to consciously recognize the unspoken pressure on men to "be the rock". Understand that this script is a cultural inheritance, not a personal mandate. When you're facing loss, give yourself explicit permission to not be okay. Your grief is not a burden to others; it's a testament to your love. Your strength is not in your silence, but in your courage to feel.

- **Grief in Action: Build a Legacy.** Grief doesn't have to be a passive state of sadness. For men, it can often be more effectively processed through action. Turn your grief into an active ritual of remembrance. Build something in their honor. Go on an annual hike on your friend's birthday and tell a story about him at the summit. Cook your mother's favorite meal and teach your children how to make it. These actions create a sacred space to process loss in a way that feels productive and honors their legacy.

- **Find Your Grief Witness.** The isolation of grief is toxic. Your mission is to find at least one person, a partner, a sibling, a trusted friend and let them witness your grief. You don't need a long, tearful conversation. You just need to break the silence. Start small. Say, "Man, I was really thinking about my dad today. I miss him." You don't need advice. You just need a witness.

- **Name the Complex Feelings.** It is okay to feel relief alongside sadness when a loved one's suffering ends. It is okay to feel anger at the unfairness of a sudden loss. It is okay to feel numb. Give yourself permission to feel these messy, contradictory emotions without judgment. Naming them is the first step to taming them. It acknowledges their existence without giving them power over you. Remember, these can be manifestations of a deeper distress, like depression, that appears differently in men.

- **Map Your New World.** When you feel "lost to the world you grew up with," it's because that world is, in fact, gone. Acknowledge that reality. The work now is not to search for the old landmarks, but to begin drawing a new map. This means building new traditions. It means strengthening the bonds with the family and friends you have left. It means creating a new sense of "home" in the world as it is now. This is not about replacing what you've lost, but about building a life that honors it while being fully present in the one you have.

Discussion Questions

1. What was the "script" for how a man should grieve that you learned from your family or community? How has that script impacted your own experiences with loss?

2. Think of a significant loss you've experienced. Did you feel you had permission to grieve openly, or did you feel an internal or external pressure to be "the strong one"?

3. Have you ever experienced "isolated grief," where you couldn't share your loss with others who understood the specific relationship? How did that isolation affect you?

4. The chapter discusses feeling relief alongside sadness. Have you ever experienced complex or contradictory emotions during a time of grief? What did that feel like, and did you feel any guilt about it?

5. What is one "active ritual" you could create to honor the memory of someone you've lost? How would that help you in your grieving process?

Chapter 4: Buried by the Grind

If there's one pressure that men rarely speak about but feel in their bones every single day, it's money. It's not the aspirational desire for more of it, though our culture certainly encourages that. It's the visceral, gut-level need for it. It's the carrying of its weight, the constant, low-grade fear of not having enough, of being seen as less of a man because of it. It's the quiet, creeping terror of failing your family financially and having that failure defines the very core of your manhood. This isn't just about economic stability; for many of us, it is a fundamental and ongoing challenge to our identity, our perceived value, and our very sense of self-worth.

From the time we are boys, we are taught a simple, powerful, and dangerous equation: a man's worth equals his provision. We learn it from the cultural ether, from the archetypes we see in movies, and from the expectations we absorb from our own families and the rest of society. The good man is the good provider. He is the one who keeps the lights on, the refrigerator full, the foundation steady. It's a noble, powerful calling. But it becomes toxic when that role as provider fuses with our identity, when our net worth becomes indistinguishable from our self-worth. We cease to be men who provide and instead become providers who happen to be men. And in that subtle shift, we set ourselves up for a life of quiet desperation, where any financial stumble feels like a complete collapse of character.

I've felt this pressure my whole life. It feels like a silent inheritance, an anxiety passed down from my father through the very atmosphere of our home. He was a good man, a hard worker, a provider in the most traditional sense of the word. But our home was wallpapered with his stress. He was a man perpetually on edge. I can still see him coming home from a long day at a job he didn't love, his broad shoulders visibly slumping with the weight of it all as he walked through the door. I can still hear the quiet, weary sighs he'd let out when he thought no one was listening. When the bills arrived in the mail, the tension in the air was a palpable, unspoken dread that hung over our dinner table like a fog.

I have a crystal-clear memory of him that has become, in many ways, my own cautionary tale. I must have been about ten years old. He was at the kitchen table, a single lamp casting a pale circle of light on a stack of envelopes. He didn't say a word, but his knuckles were white where he gripped a pen, his jaw set so tight it looked like it could crack. My mom tried to ask him something, and he just grunted, not looking up, his entire being consumed by the numbers on the pages in front of him. That image of his silent, lonely, burdened frustration became my earliest and most powerful understanding of what it meant to be a man: you carry the weight, you carry it alone, and you never, ever let anyone see the cracks in your foundation. He wasn't angry at us. He was angry at the grind. And that grind, that silent, suffocating anxiety, passed right on to me.

I didn't realize until much later that the quiet tension in that room was shaping me just as much as the words my parents spoke. My dad never sat me down to teach me about money, but I learned anyway, not from a budget sheet, but from the weight in his shoulders when the mail came.

This silent inheritance wasn't just a vague feeling; it manifested in specific, recurring scenes. I remember one summer when the central air conditioning unit in our small house died. For weeks, we lived in sweltering heat that made the vinyl kitchen chairs sticky and warped the candles on the mantle. My father, a man who already worked sixty hours a week, took on more hours on weekends, to save up for the repair. I remember seeing him come home on a Sunday afternoon, his face flushed red from the sun, his clothes stained with dirt and sweat, looking ten years older than he had that morning. He walked past me in the hallway and didn't say a word, heading straight for the shower. Later, I overheard my parents arguing in hushed, tense tones in the kitchen. "We can't keep this up," my mother said, her voice strained. "You're going to kill yourself." My father's reply was low and guttural, filled with frustration so deep it sounded like pain. "What else am I supposed to do? Tell me!" It wasn't a question seeking an answer; it was a cry of pure desperation from a man trapped in a cage of responsibility. I sat on the stairs, my ten-year-old heart pounding, and in that moment, I learned another lesson: not only does a man carry the weight alone, but the weight is unbearable, and it makes him angry and sad in a way no one knows how to fix.

I swore to myself that I would do it differently. I swore I wouldn't let that same tension appear in my own home, that my kids would never feel that same unspoken dread. Yet here I am, a man in his late 30's, living inside a pressure cooker of my own making. I'm a full-time teacher, I run a side hustle that loses money, and I work nights and weekends coaching multiple select soccer teams. Not because I'm a workaholic who loves the hustle, but because

I feel, on a primal level, that I have to. The fear of financial failure that I inherited from my father is now wired so deeply into my nervous system that I can't sit still without a corrosive guilt crawling up my spine. It's a visceral tightening in my chest, a physical unease that makes any real relaxation feel impossible, an uncontrollable anxiety that puts me into panic. It is a relentless internal voice that whispers, "If you stop, it all falls apart. You'll be a failure, just like you always feared.".

I remember a few years ago, a group of friends, all successful in their own fields, invited my wife and me out for a birthday dinner at a restaurant I knew we couldn't afford. I spent days leading up to it with a knot of anxiety in my stomach. I even checked the menu online beforehand, a secret reconnaissance mission to map out the cheapest acceptable entree and pre-calculate the damage. At the table, I could feel the familiar hum starting as everyone ordered expensive cocktails and appetizers without a second thought. I nursed a single beer, trying to make it last, and when the waiter came to take our order, I pointed to the chicken, the second cheapest thing on the menu, and tried to make my voice sound casual, like it was the thing I'd been craving all day. It's not just the bills that weigh you down. It's the unspoken comparisons, the feeling of being an imposter in your own life. You start to measure your worth not by the love in your home or the integrity of your work, but by the size of your paycheck. And every time you feel you've fallen short, the hum gets louder.

The worst part of this internal pressure is the isolation it creates within my own marriage. When I try to bring it up with my wife, it usually ends in frustration. She is a loving and supportive partner, but I don't think she fully understands the panic, the shame, the constant, demoralizing self-comparison to friends in other fields making double or triple what I make as an educator. I want to explain the knot in my stomach, but the words get stuck. How do you explain to the person you love that this isn't just about numbers on a spreadsheet, but about a perceived failure of your manhood? That it's the feeling that you are not measuring up to the unspoken standard of what a man is supposed to provide? She means well and works hard for our family but her dismissive demeanor toward the problem crushes me when I'm trying to describe a full-blown crisis of identity and family finances. This communication breakdown feels like hitting a wall, leaving me feeling even more alone in my struggle.

It was one of those nights after the kids were in bed and the house had finally fallen silent. The only light in the living room was the cold, blue-white glow of my laptop screen. I had the online banking portal open, a spreadsheet of our budget next to it, and the numbers were screaming at me. The mortgage payment was due, the car insurance had just auto drafted, and my wife's credit card balance (the only one I could see) had jumped by another several hundred dollars. It felt like trying to plug a dozen holes in a sinking boat with only my own two hands. A familiar knot tightened my gut, that corrosive mix of fear and failure. I clicked over to another tab, my fingers moving on their own, typing in phrases like "weekend coaching gigs" and "part-time jobs for teachers." Anything to feel a flicker of control.

My wife came into the room to get a glass of water, her face soft with sleep. "Still up?" she asked, her voice quiet. She glanced at the screen. "Doing the bills? I took a breath, the words catching in my throat. "Yeah. I'm… I'm worried, babe. That Visa bill is getting out of hand, and after everything else, we're going to be short again. I was thinking maybe I could pick up another coaching team in the spring to help." I turned the screen toward her, wanting her to see what I saw, to feel the same urgency. She squinted at the numbers for a moment, then gave a little sigh and a wave of her hand. "Oh, honey, don't get yourself all worked up. We always manage to figure it out." She said it with a casualness that felt like a slap. "But we're not figuring it out," I said, my voice more strained than I intended. "We're just digging a deeper hole." She just shook her head, a small, tired smile on her face. "You worry too much. It's just money. It'll be fine. Let's not talk about it tonight, okay?" She leaned over, gave me a quick kiss on the top of my head, and headed back to the bedroom, leaving me alone with the glowing screen and the crushing, silent weight of it all. In that moment, the financial problem felt secondary. The real crisis was the profound, isolating realization that I was completely on my own in the storm. Looking back, I realize she was likely trying to soothe a fear she didn't understand, while I was desperate to have my panic validated.

This experience of hiding financial fear is incredibly common among men. It's a form of "financial infidelity," where the secret isn't an affair, but the depth of our anxiety about money, often hidden for fear of being seen as a failure. This is because, for many men, our identity and our bank account are inextricably linked. Research consistently shows that men strongly associate their financial success with their self-worth and their value to their family. When money is tight, we are more likely to experience depressive symptoms and avoid seeking help because doing so feels like admitting defeat. This pressure is immense. According to a 2023 study from the American Psychological Association, over 70% of men report money as their primary source of stress. The strain is so significant that it's a major contributor to the mental health crisis among men, directly correlated with higher rates of anxiety, depression, and even suicidal ideation.

I'm not afraid of hard work; I've worked myself into the ground before and I'll do it again. It's the feeling of working so hard and still drowning that eats at a man's soul. When my finances feel like a mess (which they always seem to be), everything else starts to unravel. I withdraw from my wife. I become irritable with my kids. I obsess over every small expense. And in my darkest moments, I start to believe the world and my family would be better off without me. I have those thoughts more times than I care to admit, often triggered by something as small as an unexpected car repair or seeing a friend post vacation photos on social media. In those moments, the weight of my perceived financial failure feels unbearable, a suffocating blanket of despair.

What pulls me back from that brink is a fierce, primal refusal to lose the war. I visualize my kids' faces, their laughter, and I remind myself that they don't need a rich dad. They need a present one. They need a dad who shows them that a man's worth isn't measured by his income, but by his integrity, his effort, and his love.

To survive the grind, I had to create my own tools, tools designed not just for coping, but for healing and for fundamentally redefining my own sense of worth. The first is something I call the "Enough Tracker." This is a radical act of resistance against a culture that always screams for "more". It's not about comparing myself to others; it's about sitting down and honestly defining what enough looks like for me. Enough money in the bank to live without constant panic. Enough time in the evening to have a real conversation with my wife. Enough energy on the weekend to be truly present with my kids. Enough self-respect to stop chasing a hollow version of success and start honoring my own progress. The process was surprisingly difficult. It forced me to confront the endless loop of social comparison and the ingrained belief that my worth was tied to endless accumulation. But once I defined it, "enough" became my compass, guiding my choices away from external validation and toward internal peace. My hope is to one day, be able to reach "enough".

The second tool is a family ritual I call "Go Broke on Purpose Day". One day every month, we intentionally do something simple, free, and meaningful as a family. A hike in the state park. A picnic by the river. Building a blanket fort in the living room and telling stories with flashlights. The first time we tried it, I was anxious. I worried the kids would be bored, that it would feel cheap, that it would only serve to highlight our financial limitations. But the reality was pure joy. I'll never forget one of those days when we spent hours at a local creek, skipping rocks and building little dams out of river stones. My youngest, who is usually glued to a screen, was utterly captivated, his face alight with a genuine wonder that no expensive toy could ever replicate. That day, watching him, I realized something profound: joy doesn't have a price tag. And neither should a man's legacy.

These aren't just clever life hacks; they are evidence-based healing practices. Research consistently shows that engaging in meaningful family rituals makes families more resilient to financial stress by providing stability and building emotional security. Furthermore, even brief outdoor escapes, these "microadventures" (we will talk about these in further details later) are proven to improve our mood and reduce our levels of cortisol, the body's main stress hormone. They are deliberate acts of re-prioritization that signal to our nervous system that safety, joy, and connection are still accessible, even in the midst of the grind.

We need to have honest conversations about our financial fears. We don't have to pretend money doesn't matter. It does. But we cannot let it own our worth. To the men reading this who feel that same weight on their shoulders: your paycheck is not your identity. Your net worth is not your self-worth. We were built for more than burnout. We were built to lead, yes, but also to feel, to rest, and to be loved for who we are, not for what we earn. And no number in your bank account can ever take that away from you.

Actionable Insights for the Trail Ahead

- **Define "Enough" for Yourself.** This weekend, take 30 minutes of uninterrupted time with a notebook and honestly assess what "enough" truly means for you, not for your neighbor or your friends on social media. Write down these four headings: Financial Enough, Time Enough, Energy Enough, and

Presence Enough. Under each, write one specific, measurable goal. For example, under "Time Enough," you might write, "Enough time to eat dinner with my family five nights a week without my phone on the table." This exercise is a powerful act of defiance against "hustle culture".

- **Schedule a "Go Broke on Purpose Day."** Look at the calendar for the next month and block out one day to engage in a simple, free, and meaningful activity with your family or friends. The goal is to prioritize presence over spending. To make it real, create a simple itinerary: "10 AM: Walk the dog at the state park. 12 PM: Picnic lunch we packed from home. 2 PM: Living room blanket fort and a movie." Afterward, take five minutes to journal about how the experience felt. This practice helps rewire your brain to find value and joy in connection rather than consumption.

- **Start Small with Microadventures.** You don't need a grand expedition to feel the benefits of nature. This week, commit to one 20-minute microadventure. This could be a walk in a local park on your lunch break, exploring a new neighborhood on foot after dinner, or simply watching the sunrise from your backyard with a cup of coffee. This small disruption to your routine is a proven and effective way to reduce stress and cultivate presence.

- **Initiate an Honest Conversation about Money.** Find a trusted partner or friend and schedule a time to have an honest conversation about your financial fears. Use "I" statements to express your feelings without blame ("I feel anxious about our savings when I think about the future" instead of "You spend too much money"). Sharing this burden is a courageous act that can bring immense relief and is a crucial step in building deeper, more authentic relationships.

- **Challenge the "Wealth Equals Worth" Narrative.** Actively notice when you are comparing your financial situation to others. This often happens unconsciously while scrolling social media or talking with friends. When you catch yourself doing this, consciously redirect your thoughts to what you value internally about yourself, your character, your integrity, your role as a father or friend, your effort. Remember that your worth is inherent and not for sale.

Discussion Questions

- The author describes inheriting his father's financial stress as a "silent inheritance." What unspoken burdens or beliefs about money, work, or success have you received from your family?

- How does the "fear of failing financially" manifest in your own life? Do you feel guilt when you are resting or not being productive?

- The chapter highlights that for many men, financial success is tied to identity and self-worth. How has this societal narrative influenced your own self-perception, career choices, or relationships?

- The "Enough Tracker" and "Go Broke on Purpose Day" are presented as healing practices. What does "enough" truly look like for

you, beyond external comparisons? What is one free, meaningful activity you could do with your family or friends this month?

Chapter 5: Beyond the Grind

Let's just say it: hustle culture is killing us. For most of our lives, we have been fed a pervasive and damaging lie. The lie says that a real man grinds 24/7, that he never complains, and that his worth is measured by his output. We have been taught that success is directly proportional to exhaustion and that if you are not constantly, relentlessly busy, you are not doing enough. This lie, deeply ingrained in our societal fabric, whispers that "more" is always the answer. It tells us that rest is a luxury for the weak and that true worth is found in the endless, punishing pursuit of external achievements.

I internalized this toxic message early on. I saw it modeled in my father's constant stress and his inability to rest. I felt it in my own desperate need to prove myself after the shame of my first marriage ending. The societal messages were everywhere, in media that glorified entrepreneurs who "slept when they were dead," and in the unspoken expectations within my own community that a man always "provides" and always "figures it out". The promise was always that if I just pushed harder, hustled more, and filled every single waking hour, I would finally feel successful. I would finally feel enough.

But here is the truth: most of us are just exhausted. We are not lazy or unmotivated, just completely and utterly done. I have been there, and honestly, I still visit that place often. I live a life that, on paper, looks like the epitome of the grind. I am a full-time teacher, I coach multiple select soccer teams, I launched a business, and I am parenting three kids, all while carrying the quiet, emotional weight of unresolved trauma. For years, I believed that if I just pushed harder, I would finally feel the satisfaction I was chasing. I did not. I just felt hollow.

This hollowness was not a simple lack of joy; it was a profound and cavernous emptiness, a sense that despite all the frantic activity, nothing truly meaningful was being sustained. It manifested as a constant, low-grade anxiety, a feeling of being perpetually behind, even when I was ahead on my to-do list. My mind would race, unable to quiet itself. Sleep became elusive, and when it came, it was rarely restorative. I was a ghost in my own life, physically present, but mentally and emotionally a million miles away, unable to fully engage with my family or find pleasure in the things I once loved.

I remember one specific Saturday a few years ago that perfectly captures this state. I had been working seventy-hour weeks, teaching all day, coaching in the evenings, and trying to build my side business late into the night. My wife had planned a family outing to a local apple orchard. It was supposed to be a perfect fall day. But I was a wreck. I was so physically and mentally depleted that every interaction felt like a monumental effort. At the orchard, while my kids laughed and ran through the rows of trees, I just stood there, a profound sense of disconnection washing over me. I was watching my life from a distance, like it was a movie starring someone else. Later that day, my youngest son, excited about the apples we'd picked, asked if I would help him make a pie. My immediate, gut-level reaction wasn't joy or love; it was a surge of pure, unadulterated irritation. Another demand. Another thing I have to do. I snapped at him, my voice sharper than I intended: "Not right now, buddy. I'm exhausted." The look of hurt and confusion on his face was a gut punch. I had become a man who was too tired to make a pie with his son on a Saturday afternoon. The grind hadn't just stolen my time; it had stolen my capacity for joy.

I know I am not alone in this. Burnout is not a personal weakness or a moral failing. It is a signal from your mind and body that you have pushed past your sustainable limits. And for many of us, that signal has been blaring, unheeded, for years. While the majority of workers in America now report experiencing burnout, it often manifests differently in men. Instead of the overt sadness we typically associate with depression, male burnout often appears as anger, a short fuse, irritability, irrationality, and social withdrawal. When men are conditioned from boyhood to suppress their emotions and dismiss traits perceived as "feminine," our mental health suffers, and our distress comes out sideways. I remember snapping at my kids over the smallest infractions, feeling a surge of disproportionate anger that I could not explain. My wife would gently ask what was wrong, and I would just grunt or retreat into myself, unable to articulate the simmering frustration that felt like it was consuming me from the inside out. This is the classic male burnout pattern. We withdraw from our wives, our children, and our friendships, becoming dangerously isolated because vulnerability feels too threatening.

We do not just need a break from this cycle. We need a new way of living. For me, that new way of living begins in the pre-dawn darkness, at 3:45 AM. I wake up to work out, not because I am a fitness fanatic, but because it is the only quiet time in my day that is entirely and unapologetically mine. The decision to start this routine was not born from discipline, but from desperation. I was so overwhelmed, so hollow, that I knew something had to fundamentally change. I needed a space that was entirely my own, free from the demands and expectations of the world.

That quiet, solitary time, before anyone else in my house is awake, has become my sanctuary. The early morning sweat is not just physical; it is a mental and emotional release. It is a primal act of self-care that grounds me, clears the mental fog, and reminds me of my own agency before the demands of the day can begin to chip away at it. It is a deliberate act of choosing myself first, so that I have something left to give to everyone else.

This is my personal sanctuary, but the principle is universal. For another man, it might be a quiet cup of coffee on the back porch before the sun comes up, a ten-minute meditation practice, or an evening walk after the kids are in bed. The key is to find what genuinely offers you that vital self-reconnection and to protect that time fiercely. This anchor habit is supported by other small, sustainable practices. Weekend hikes with my family, with no screens and no deadlines. Just us, the dirt under our shoes, and the feeling of our lungs working. It is writing these words, not to go viral or become famous, but because the process of translating my internal chaos into sentences on a page heals something in me. These habits are not always graceful or glamorous, but they are sustainable. Small habits matter more than big goals. You do not need a 90-day life makeover plan; start with the basics like drinking water, getting sunlight, and walking for twenty minutes a day. These seemingly insignificant actions accumulate into significant shifts in well-being.

One of the hardest and most important lessons for me to unlearn was that rest is not a reward; it is a nonnegotiable component of a healthy life. In a culture that glorifies the grind, men often feel guilty for resting, viewing it as unproductive or lazy. But you are not a machine. You do not need to prove your worth by breaking yourself down. Prioritizing sleep and downtime are vital for recovery, mood regulation, and preventing burnout. This requires setting clear boundaries, which are personal limits that define what we are willing to accept from others and from ourselves. Setting boundaries is an act of self-respect that protects our mental health, enhances self-esteem, and allows us to create a healthy work life balance.

I still struggle with this. I still overcommit and find myself saying, "I'll slow down next month". The process of unlearning the grind is a continuous battle. A while back, I was asked to take on an additional coaching role that would have meant even more late nights and weekend commitments. The old programming in my head, the voice of the hustle, screamed at me to say yes, driven by the fear of missing an opportunity. But I paused. I remembered the hollowness. And for the first time in a long time, I said, "No, I can't take that on right now. My family and my current commitments need my full presence". The immediate impact was a wave of relief, a feeling of protecting something precious. It was an uncomfortable but powerful act of self-preservation.

This is what it comes down to. Our kids do not need perfect, exhausted fathers; they need present ones. Our partners do not need million-dollar providers who are emotionally bankrupt; they need men who know how to breathe, who show up emotionally, and who still have something left in the tank at the end of the day. The world will always ask more of you. It is your job to decide what matters most and to protect it with fierce boundaries. We do not win this game by pushing harder. We win by refusing to let the grind steal the best parts of us.

Actionable Insights for the Trail Ahead

- **Identify Your Burnout Triggers.** Pay close attention this week to the specific situations, thoughts, or demands that lead to feelings of exhaustion, irritability, or the urge to withdraw. Is it a particular meeting at work? A certain time of day? A specific financial worry? Keep a "burnout journal" on your phone or in a notebook for a few days to track these patterns and gain crucial self-awareness.

- **Implement One "Sanctuary" Habit.** Choose one small, sustainable self-care habit to implement as your personal sanctuary. This should be something that is just for you. Start with something so small you cannot say no to it, like five minutes of quiet time with your coffee before anyone else is awake, a 15-minute walk alone after work, or listening to one full album without distractions. Schedule it and protect it.

- **Define and Defend One Boundary.** Identify one area in your life where you need to set a clearer limit, for example, not checking work emails after 7

PM, saying no to a social commitment you do not have the energy for, or protecting your weekend mornings for family. This week, practice saying "no" to one request that would push you past your capacity. Remember, setting a boundary is an act of self-respect and self-preservation.

- **Prioritize Rest as Essential.** Shift your mindset from viewing rest as a reward for hard work to seeing it as a non-negotiable component of your well-being. Schedule downtime on your calendar and treat it as seriously as you would an important work appointment. This could be a 20-minute nap, an hour of reading a book, or simply a night with a firm "lights out" time.

- **Cultivate Self-Compassion.** When you get off track, practice self-compassion instead of self-judgment. Acknowledge your struggles with kindness, recognizing that imperfection is part of the human experience. Ask yourself, "What would I tell a good friend in this exact situation?" and then apply that same kindness and gentle advice to yourself.

Discussion Questions

- The author critiques "hustle culture". What specific societal messages or personal beliefs have driven you to "grind" in your own life? What has been the cost to your well-being?

- Male burnout is described as often manifesting as anger, irritability, and social withdrawal. Have you experienced these symptoms? How do they impact your relationships?

- The author's 3:45 AM workout is a non-negotiable rhythm. What is one small, consistent habit you could implement that would serve as a "sanctuary" or a deliberate act of self-care?

- The chapter emphasizes that "Rest isn't earned. It's essential" What does this statement mean to you, and how does it challenge your ingrained beliefs about productivity and worth?

Chapter 6: Brotherhood in the Wild

Here is a truth that I didn't fully understand until I was well into my thirties: most men are profoundly lonely. It's not necessarily the kind of loneliness that comes from physical solitude, although that happens too. It's a quieter, more insidious kind of loneliness, the kind you can feel in a crowded room, at a party, or even sitting on the couch next to your spouse. It's the loneliness of being surrounded by people yet feeling completely and utterly unknown. It's the ache of having a thousand acquaintances but no one to call in the middle of the night.

You have work friends you chat with by the coffee machine, colleagues who know what projects you're working on but have no idea about the anxiety that's keeping you up at night. You have a group text with your college buddies that pings with a steady stream of memes, sports highlights, and inside jokes that feel like echoes from a different lifetime, a time when your connection felt real and effortless. You have "how's life?" conversations over beers where everything is kept safely, carefully, on the surface. "Life's good, man. Busy, but good. How about you?" "Same, same. Can't complain." It's a script we all follow, a conversational dance of mutual non-disclosure.

We talk around our lives, but we rarely talk about them. Deep down, there is an aching emptiness, a sense of being perpetually on the outside looking in, because you know, with a certainty that settles deep in your bones, that no one has heard the full story. Not even close.

For years, I assumed this was just the natural, inevitable progression of adult life. You grow up, you get busy, you have kids, you hustle, and the deep, meaningful friendships of your youth fade into the background like an old photograph. My core group of adult close friends is now scattered across the country, from California to Nashville to St. Louis. We keep our group chat alive, and I'm grateful for it, but it's a space for banter, not for bearing your soul. It's for sharing a funny picture of our kids, debating a bad call in last night's game, or planning a fantasy football draft. It is a lifeline to a shared past, but it often feels insufficient for the present.

I can remember countless times sitting with my phone in my hand, my thumb hovering over the keyboard, wanting to type out something real. There were nights I'd be awake at 2 a.m., the weight of financial stress pressing down on my chest, and I would open that group chat. I'd type, "Man, I'm really struggling with money lately. It's eating me alive." And then I would stare at the words on the screen, a lump forming in my throat. The fears would rush in, a tidal wave of self-doubt. What if they don't respond? I'd think. What if they think it's too heavy, too much of a burden? What if they just reply with a thumbs-up emoji or a stupid GIF? The fear of being seen as weak, as needy, or of simply having my vulnerability met with silence, was a powerful and paralyzing barrier. And so, I would delete the message, every single time. Instead, I'd send a meme I'd saved from earlier. It was easier. It was safer. It kept me in the club. And it kept me completely alone. Eventually, I stopped trying. I started to believe that something was fundamentally broken in me, that my yearning for a deeper connection was a flaw I needed to suppress.

But I'm not broken. I'm not the problem. We're in a collective crisis. Recent data from the American Survey Center reveals a startling "friendship recession" among American men. In 2021, nearly one in five men reported not having a single close friend, a fivefold increase since 1990. Richard Reeves, author of Of Boys and Men, identifies this as a primary driver of the struggles the modern male is facing. Furthermore, while men and women report similar rates of feeling lonely, there is a significant gender gap in how we seek emotional support. One Pew

Research Center study found that only 21% of men in the U.S. say they get emotional support from friends on a regular basis, compared to 41% of women. This data highlights a crucial point: men may feel lonely at similar rates, but we are far less likely to seek or receive the connection that could alleviate it. I know that I personally am guilty of not seeking that connection, despite acknowledging the need for it and giving that same advice to others.

This is not a social inconvenience; it is a full-blown public health emergency. The U.S. Surgeon General has issued an advisory on the devastating health effects of loneliness and isolation, which are now linked to a significantly increased risk for heart disease, strokes, and dementia. Esteemed researchers from a landmark Harvard study concluded that chronic loneliness is as harmful to our long-term health as smoking fifteen cigarettes a day. Let that sink in. We have meticulously built lives where we are surrounded by people but are emotionally starving to death in plain sight. We convince ourselves that needing others is weakness, when in fact, it's a fundamental human need as critical as food or water. And the consequences are dire. While men make up just under half the U.S. population, we now account for nearly 80% of all suicides. The lack of deep, platonic intimacy is a significant contributor to this silent epidemic.

This abstract crisis became intensely personal for me on a trekking trip in the Andes mountains of Peru. I went with three of my closest friends. Well, they are close to me; I often wonder and doubt I fall into the same category for them. They were all in great shape, successful in their careers, and by all external measures, had their lives completely together.

I, on the other hand, was a wreck. The trip came just a month after the school shooting at my workplace, and I was still reeling. My body hadn't recovered, and my mind was a numb, buzzing mess of unprocessed trauma. I was physically out of shape, constantly sick with altitude-induced nausea and pounding headaches, and on the second day, my feet were already covered in blisters so raw that every step was an exercise in pain management. I felt like the weak link, a burden, and that feeling amplified the deep inner shame I already carried. My internal monologue was a relentless chorus of self-criticism: You're holding them back. You shouldn't have come. You're weak.

I remember one afternoon with painful clarity. We were on a steep ascent to a mountain pass at over 15,000 feet. The air was thin and sharp, and every breath felt like I was sipping through a narrow straw. My head was pounding in rhythm with my frantic heartbeat. My friends, seasoned hikers, were moving ahead with a steady, rhythmic pace. I was falling further and further behind, stopping every fifty feet, bent over my trekking poles, gasping for air that wasn't there. The shame was an emotional weight, heavier than my pack. I was convinced they were annoyed, waiting for me up ahead, silently cursing my lack of fitness. I was about to yell for them to go on without me when I looked up. They had all stopped. They weren't looking back at me with impatience. They were just waiting, looking out at the vast, silent valley, giving me the space to suffer without making it a spectacle. When I finally caught up, sucking wind that wasn't there and embarrassed, one of them, just clapped me on the shoulder. "Brutal, isn't it?" he said with a small smile. And that was it. No judgment. No condescending encouragement. Just a simple, shared acknowledgement of the struggle.

But my friends never made me feel that way. Not for a single second. When my pace slowed to a crawl, they sometimes slowed with me. When I needed to stop and catch my breath, they stopped, no questions asked. They walked beside me. There were no jokes at my expense.

There was no pressure to keep up. There was just their quiet, steady presence. That non-verbal support was more powerful than any words of encouragement could have ever been. It was a physical manifestation of acceptance that directly counteracted the screaming inner voice that told me, "You're weak. You're holding them back. You don't belong here.". Their quiet presence was salt on a wound I didn't even know was bleeding so badly.

The sensory details of that support are still vivid in my mind: the rhythmic crunch of their boots on the trail next to mine, a sound that said, we're with you; the shared silence punctuated only by our labored breaths at 15,000 feet; the simple feeling of a hand on my shoulder when I stumbled on a loose rock. It wasn't about what they said, but what they did. That trail, those mountains, and those men held space for me without ever needing me to explain my pain.

The clearest moment of this bond didn't happen on a windswept mountain pass, but in a small, noisy restaurant in Aguas Calientes, the town at the foot of Machu Picchu. We were showered and clean for the first time in days and sat around a wobbly wooden table. The air was thick with the smell of roasted chicken and garlic, and the clinking of beer bottles felt like a symphony. I remember looking at my friends, their faces relaxed and ruddy from the sun and wind and feeling a sense of peace so profound it was almost dizzying. The aches in my legs and the raw spots on my feet were still there, but they felt less like injuries and more like souvenirs from a battle we had won together.

The conversation was easy, punctuated by laughter that was loud and genuine. We weren't talking about our feelings or having some deep, emotional breakthrough. We were rehashing the trip, turning our shared misery into legend. One of my friends raised his glass. "To Rob's blisters," he said with a wide grin. "The real MVP of this trek. I think they deserve their own passport stamp." Everyone roared with laughter, and instead of the familiar hot flush of shame I would have once felt, I just laughed with them, the sound coming from deep in my belly. In that moment, the joke wasn't at my expense; it was a celebration of my struggle. It was an acknowledgment that they had seen me at my weakest, literally limping my way through the journey, and not only had they not judged me, they were now raising a glass to it. It was their way of saying, "We saw you suffer, and you were still one of us." That easy, shared laughter, echoing in that little Peruvian restaurant, was one of the most powerful forms of acceptance I have ever known.

That trip felt like something ancient, like what men have done for centuries: journeying together, facing the challenges of nature, and wrestling with their inner lives out on the rocks and ridgelines. Modern life rarely gives us that. This is what experts call "shoulder-to-shoulder" connection. Men often find it easier to connect emotionally and build intimacy when they are engaged in a shared activity, rather than in direct, face-to-face emotional disclosure. The shared challenge, the common goal, reduces the pressure of direct vulnerability and allows intimacy to emerge organically through mutual reliance. It's an indirect pathway to connection that bypasses our ingrained discomfort with overt emotional expression.

What happened in Peru for me was medicine. We need more of that kind of healing. We don't just need more guys to grab a beer with. We need men who will walk beside us up the literal and metaphorical mountains of our lives. Men who won't flinch when we start to break down. Men who understand that sometimes, the absolute best thing you can do for a brother is just stay beside him in the struggle.

The transition back to normal life is hard. The practical barriers are real. It's easy to slip back into old patterns of isolation. But I have tasted something better. I have seen what real brotherhood looks like. You don't have to go to Peru to find it. But you do have to go somewhere. The antidote to loneliness isn't more noise or more distraction. It's intentional connection.

Actionable Insights for the Trail Ahead

- **Recognize the Depth of Your Loneliness.** Take a moment this week to honestly assess your own level of connection with a "Connection Audit." On a piece of paper, write down three categories: Work Colleagues, Old Friends (long distance), and Local Friends. Under each, list the names of the men you have the most contact with. Now, next to each name, answer this question honestly: "Could I call this person at 10 PM on a Tuesday if I were in a personal crisis?" This isn't a judgment; it's a diagnostic tool. The goal is to get a clear, unflinching look at the real state of your support system. Acknowledging the gap between the number of people you *know* and the number of people who truly *know you* is the first courageous step.

- **Be the Initiator (With a Script).** Don't wait for others to reach out. Most men are waiting for someone else to break the silence. Be that person. The fear of awkwardness is real, so use a low-risk script. This week, pick one friend you haven't seen in a while and send them one of the following texts:

1. **The Shared Memory:** "Hey, I was just thinking about that ridiculous time we [insert specific, funny memory]. Hope you're doing well, man." This requires no immediate action from him but re-establishes a positive connection.

2. **The Low-Stakes Ask:** "I'm grabbing a coffee/going for a walk this Saturday morning at [place/time]. Any chance you're free and want to join?" This is a specific, easy-to-decline invitation that removes the pressure.

3. **The Direct Approach:** "It's been too long. We need to catch up. What does your schedule look like in the next couple of weeks?"

- **Embrace "Shoulder-to-Shoulder" Connection.** Plan an activity where you are doing something *alongside* a friend, not just sitting across from them. The power of this approach is that it creates a "third thing" to focus on the project, the trail, the game, which diffuses the intensity and allows conversation to emerge more naturally. Go beyond the basics:

1. **Build something:** Assemble a piece of furniture, build a fire pit, or work on a small project in the garage. The shared task creates an instant bond.

2. **Learn something:** Take a one-day class together, like a cooking class, a basic mechanics workshop, or even a martial art.

3. **Explore something:** Go to a museum you've never been to, check out a new brewery or record store, or take a drive to a nearby town you don't know.

- **Explore Intentional Male Spaces.** Consider seeking out environments specifically designed to foster male connection and vulnerability. This isn't about finding more drinking buddies; it's about finding a safe container for authentic conversation. Look into local

- **Men's Sheds,** which are community spaces for men to connect through shared activities or use Meetup to find groups centered on a hobby you enjoy, like a hiking club or a photography group. A good men's group isn't just a gripe session; it's a place to practice the skills of listening and sharing with men who are on a similar journey.

- **Practice Active Listening and Presence.** When a friend does share something real with you, give them the invaluable gift of your full, undivided attention. Put your phone away. Listen to understand, not just to respond. Practice the 3-Second Rule: after he finishes talking, pause and take a full, silent breath before you respond. This prevents you from interrupting and shows you are truly processing what he said. Then, instead of giving advice, offer validation: "Man, that sounds incredibly frustrating," or "I can see why you'd be angry about that".

- **Say Something Real (Using the Vulnerability Ladder).** Sharing something genuinely vulnerable feels risky, so don't start at the top of the ladder. Practice with a low-stakes topic.

1. **Level 1 (The Frustration):** Share a simple, relatable frustration. "Man, work has been draining lately. The pressure on this project is getting to me."

2. **Level 2 (The Worry):** Share a small, forward-looking concern. "I'm a little worried about [an upcoming family event, a financial decision, one of the kids' struggles]."

3. **Level 3 (The Deeper Feeling):** If the trust is there, share something more significant. "I've been feeling pretty lonely lately," or "I've been thinking a lot about my dad, and it's been tough."

- **Prioritize Offline Connection.** While digital tools can help maintain distant friendships, make a conscious effort to prioritize face-to-face interactions. Make a concrete plan. Look at your calendar for the next three months and schedule one "anchor event" with your closest friends like an annual camping trip, a weekend to meet in a city halfway between you, or a daylong hike. Then, schedule one smaller, local meetup per month. Putting these on the calendar makes them real and non-negotiable.

Discussion Questions

- The author describes feeling "profoundly lonely" even when surrounded by people. Can you relate to this feeling of emotional isolation despite social interaction? What does it feel like for you?

- The chapter highlights the "friendship recession" among men. What factors do you believe contribute to the decline of deep male friendships in adulthood?

- The Peru trip demonstrated the power of "shoulder-to-shoulder" connection. What "shoulder-to-shoulder" activities do you currently engage in, or could you initiate, that might foster deeper bonds with your friends?

- How does the fear of being seen as "needy" or "weak" impact your willingness to seek or deepen friendships? How can you begin to challenge this internal barrier?

Chapter 7: Sustaining Brotherhood

If you asked most men how many real friends they have, men they can be totally, unapologetically honest with, without the usual armor and ego, the list would be shockingly short. For many of us, it is a list of one. Or zero. In Chapter 6, we explored this pervasive reality of male loneliness and the "friendship recession" that is quietly devastating our collective well-being. My transformative trip to Peru was a powerful reminder of what is possible. It was a taste of the lifesaving power of brotherhood forged through shared struggle, a connection built not on grand speeches, but on quiet, unwavering presence. But here is the brutal truth: knowing we need that connection and actually finding and nurturing it in the relentless chaos of adult life are two very different things. It is one thing to experience the clarity of a mountaintop moment, and another entirely to maintain that connection back in the valley, amidst the daily grind of mortgages, deadlines, and parenting.

The practical barriers are formidable. We are all busy. Schedules are packed. We move, change jobs, and have kids. The old assumption that "needing others is weakness," a central theme of the armor we are taught to wear, still whispers in the back of our minds. It is hard to combat the ingrained belief that we should handle everything ourselves, that reaching out to a friend is just burdening them with our problems. So, how do we bridge that gap? How do we move from a single, powerful experience of connection to a life that is rich with it? The answer is not a simple life hack. It requires intentionality. It requires practice. Adult friendships do not just happen; they are built and sustained, one deliberate act at a time.

As we get older, the built-in structures that fostered friendship like school, sports teams, and college dorms disappear. To succeed, we must become strategists, actively identifying and overcoming the barriers that stand in our way.

Overcoming the Five Great Barriers to Male Friendship

1. The Barrier of Time Scarcity

Our lives are packed to the breaking point. The very idea of "making time" for friends can feel like just another exhausting item on an already overwhelming to-do list. This is not just about being busy; it is about the guilt that modern culture instills in us for any "unproductive" time.

I remember a few years ago, an old friend was passing through town for a night. He texted me, "Hey man, in town for work. Free to grab a beer tonight?" My immediate, gut-level reaction was a surge of joy. I hadn't seen him in years. But that joy was immediately crushed by a wave of obligation. It was a Tuesday. I had a stack of papers to grade, my son had soccer practice I was coaching, my wife was exhausted from her own long day, and the thought of adding one more thing to the evening felt physically impossible. I typed out, "Man, I'd love to, but I'm swamped tonight. Rain check?" He replied with a quick, "No worries, man. Next time." But we both knew "next time" was a fiction. The opportunity was lost. I spent the rest of the night feeling a low-grade sense of guilt and loss. I had chosen the urgent over the important, and in doing so, I had let a real, life-giving connection wither on the vine. This is the tyranny of the packed schedule; it convinces us that friendship is a luxury we can't afford.

The Strategy: Integration Over Addition. The solution is not to magically create more hours in the day. It is to integrate connections into the routines you already have. Instead of seeing friendship as a separate event you have to schedule, weave it into the fabric of your life. Turn your solo commute into a time to call a friend. Invite a buddy to join your gym session or a weekend run. Combine a family trip to the park with another family. These regular, shorter interactions are often more sustainable and more powerful than a single, grand reunion every two years.

2. The Barrier of Awkwardness and Fear

After years, or even decades, of emotional suppression, initiating a deeper conversation or suggesting a get-together can feel incredibly vulnerable. The internal monologue of fear can be paralyzing:

What if he says no? What if it is weird? What if he thinks I am strange for even asking?

This is the same fear that kept my own fingers hovering over my phone, unable to send a text that was actually real.

I have another friend I've known since we were kids. We live in the same town, and we see each other every few months. Our conversations are always the same comfortable rehash of work, kids, and sports. A while back, I was going through a particularly rough patch. I felt a deep need to talk to someone who knew me before all the adult armor went up. I picked up my phone to text him, thinking maybe we could go for a hike, a place where a real conversation might happen. But I froze. What would I even say? "Hey, wanna go for a walk and talk about our feelings?" It sounded absurd in my own head, like a line from a bad movie. I could picture his confused reply. The fear of that awkwardness, of disrupting the comfortable but shallow script of our friendship, was so intense that I put the phone down and never sent the text. I chose the familiar loneliness over the risk of an awkward connection.

The Strategy: Start with "Shoulder to Shoulder." The most effective antidote to this awkwardness is the principle we learned in Peru. Plan an activity where you are doing something alongside a friend, not just sitting across from them in a sterile, face-to-face interview. Go fishing. Work on a car together. Play a round of golf. Tackle a project in the garage. The shared activity becomes the comfortable container for the connection, allowing intimacy to emerge organically. Remember, most men are likely feeling the same way you are, secretly hoping someone else will be brave enough to initiate.

3. The Barrier of the "Weakness" Mindset

This is the most powerful internal obstacle. It is the inherited belief we dissected in Chapter 1: the belief that needing others, admitting loneliness, or seeking support is a betrayal of the masculine ideal of the stoic, self-reliant man.

This mindset is so deeply ingrained it can feel like a law of nature. For years, when I was struggling with the lingering trauma from my EMS days, my wife would repeatedly urge me to talk to one of my close friends about it. "They're your friends," she'd say. "They love you. They'll want to help." I knew she was right on a logical level, but on a visceral, gut level, the idea felt impossible. It felt like a fundamental failure. My internal script, a voice that sounded a lot like my grandfather, would say, "A man handles his business. Don't burden other people with your problems." To admit my struggle felt like I would be handing them a written confession of my own inadequacy. So, I kept quiet, choosing the heavy burden of silent suffering over what I perceived as the profound shame of asking for help.

The Strategy: Reframe Strength. This requires a conscious and deliberate redefinition of strength. True strength is not isolation; it is the courage to build an interdependent network of support. It is recognizing that we are stronger together. The most practical way to do this is to model the behavior yourself. Be the first to "go first". Share a small, genuine struggle with a trusted friend. When you offer a piece of your own vulnerability, you give other men permission to do the same. You actively deconstruct the harmful narrative that self-reliance means suffering alone.

4. The Barrier of Geographic Drift

It is an unavoidable fact of modern life that friends move. They take jobs in other cities, they move to be closer to family, or life simply pulls them in different directions. Friendships that are not actively maintained will naturally wither from this lack of proximity. The casual, easy connection that came from living in the same town is replaced by a logistical challenge that requires real effort to overcome.

One of my best friends from my time as a teacher in my previous district, moved to North Carolina a few years ago. We had been inseparable at work, grabbing lunch together, covering each other's classes, decompressing on Friday afternoons about the insanity of our weeks. When he left, we made all the usual promises: "We'll talk all the time. We'll do a yearly trip." For the first few months, we did. We had a couple of long phone calls, catching up on his new life and my old one. But then, life got in the way. A scheduled call would get pushed because one of our kids got sick. The weekend he was supposed to visit got canceled because of a work conflict. The calls became less frequent, then they became texts, and then, eventually, they became just the occasional liking of each other's posts on social media. The bond that had felt so solid and essential was eroded by distance, not because of a lack of love, but a lack of intention. The drift is silent and slow, and you often don't realize how far apart you've floated until you look up and the other shore is no longer in sight.

The Strategy: Be Deliberate with Distance. Technology can be a powerful tool, but it can also be a lazy substitute for real connection. Use it strategically. Schedule regular video calls where you can actually see each other's faces. Start a virtual book club or a fantasy football league that requires regular, meaningful communication. More importantly, be intentional about planning in-person meetups, even if it is just once a year. That annual camping trip or weekend get-together becomes a powerful anchor that reinforces the bond and gives you something to look forward to.

5. The Barrier of Shifting Life Stages

The nature of our social needs and available time changes dramatically as we move through life. The friend you stayed up all night with in college may not be the friend who understands the exhaustion of being a new father. Being the first in your group to get married, or the last to have kids, can be an incredibly lonely experience. Your realities diverge, and the old common ground can feel like a distant country.

When my wife and I had our youngest son, I was in my mid-thirties, and most of my close friends were past the diaper-and-sleepless-nights phase. Their kids were in elementary school, and their weekends were filled with soccer games and birthday parties. My weekends were a blur of feedings, naps, and a level of exhaustion I had forgotten existed. I remember trying to talk to a good friend about how overwhelmed I was, how the sleep deprivation was making me feel crazy. He listened, but he couldn't really relate. He just said, "Yeah man, that stage is tough. It gets better!" It was meant to be encouraging, but it felt dismissive. It made me feel like my current struggle was just a phase to endure, not a reality to be shared. Our life stages were out of sync, and it created a gap that our shared history couldn't quite bridge. It was no one's fault; it was just a reality that left me feeling more isolated in my new role as a father of a newborn. This was really true being an 18-year-old dad and everyone you know was still in high school and going off to college. It was hard to find anyone who could relate.

The Strategy: Adapt and Expand. Friendships must be allowed to evolve. You may need to find new ways to connect with long-standing friends that align with your current life demands. At the same time, do not be afraid to seek out new connections with men who are in a similar life stage. This might mean joining a parenting group, getting to know the other dads on the sidelines of your kid's soccer game, or connecting with neighbors. Expanding your circle does not mean you are replacing your old friends; it means you are building a more robust and adaptable support network for the man you are today.

The Art of Long-Term Friendship Maintenance

Beyond just initiating connection, building a brotherhood that lasts a lifetime requires consistent effort. It is a practice, not a destination.

A man I know, let's call him Ben, felt the profound sting of loneliness after his kids left for college. His old friends were scattered, and he realized his entire social life had revolved around his family. He decided to take a small, terrifying step and join a local men's running club, something he had always wanted to try. At first, it was just about the miles. The conversation was light, focused on pace and training tips. But soon, on the long, quiet weekend runs, the conversations naturally shifted. They talked about stressful jobs, aging parents, and challenges in their marriages. He found a new sense of camaraderie and accountability, realizing that the shared physical challenge had created a safe container for an emotional honesty he had not anticipated. It was not forced; it simply emerged from the shared effort and consistent presence.

Ben's story reveals the core principles of sustaining brotherhood:

- **Cultivate Consistent "Touchpoints."** Like Ben's running club, find ways to integrate small, regular interactions. This could be a weekly text exchange about a shared interest, a monthly walk, or a standing coffee date. Consistency builds trust and demonstrates that the friendship is a priority.

- **Practice Proactive Empathy.** Do not just wait for a friend to be in crisis. Pay attention. Check in regularly with open-ended questions that invite deeper sharing. If you know a friend has a big work presentation, text them good luck beforehand. If you know their kid was sick, follow up a few days later to see how they are doing. This shows you care and that you are listening to their life.

- **Shared Vulnerability (Gradually).** While "shoulder to shoulder" activities reduce pressure, truly deep friendships require some level of emotional disclosure. Start small, sharing a genuine feeling with a trusted friend. Instead of "I'm fine," try "I've been feeling a bit overwhelmed with work lately," or "I'm actually a little worried about X". Observe how they respond. The ones who meet your vulnerability with empathy and presence are your people.

- **Offer and Accept Support Reciprocally.** Friendship is a two-way street. Be willing to offer practical help and a nonjudgmental ear when a friend needs it. Equally important, you must practice the strength of receiving support when you need it. For many men, this is the harder part. Accepting help requires humility and trust. It reinforces the bond and is a powerful rejection of the "lone wolf" mentality.

- **Celebrate and Acknowledge.** Life is busy but take the time to celebrate your friends' successes and milestones. Acknowledge when they have navigated a tough week. A simple text of congratulations or a quick call to say, "I appreciate you," strengthens the bond in ways that cannot be overstated.

Most of us do not need more advice. We need more friends. Men who will walk beside us, not to fix us, but just to keep going together. The trail to wholeness is not meant to be walked alone.

Actionable Insights for the Trail Ahead

- **Identify Your Personal Barriers.** Take an honest look at the five barriers discussed in this chapter: Time Scarcity, Fear/Awkwardness, the "Weakness" Mindset, Geographic Drift, and Shifting Life Stages. Which one is the single biggest obstacle for you right now? Identifying it is the first step to creating a specific strategy to overcome it. This week, write down that barrier and brainstorm three small, practical actions you can take to counteract it.

- **Schedule Your "Touchpoints."** Look at your calendar for the next month. Where can you schedule one small, consistent point of connection with a friend you want to invest in? Make it a recurring event, even if it is just a 15-minute phone call every other Friday on your drive home from work. Put it on the calendar as you would any other important appointment. The consistency is more important than the duration.

- **Practice Proactive Empathy This Week.** Think of one friend you have not heard from in a while. Send them a text that goes beyond the generic "How's it going?". Ask a specific question that shows you are thinking of them and their life. For example: "Hey, I was just thinking about that big project you were stressed about at work. How did it all turn out?" or "Saw the pictures from your family trip, looked amazing. What was the best part?".

- **Practice Accepting Support.** The next time a friend offers to help you with something, even something small, your default may be to say, "No, I got it". This week, practice the strength of accepting. Say, "You know what, that would be a huge help. Thank you". Notice how it feels to receive support and let someone else carry a piece of the load. This is a powerful rejection of the "lone wolf" mentality.

- **Take One Small, Vulnerable Step.** Building on the idea of saying something real, identify one small, honest feeling you can share with a trusted friend this week. It could be as simple as, "Man, I've been feeling pretty burned out lately," or "I'm actually a little nervous about this upcoming family event". This is a single rep in the exercise of building a stronger, more authentic friendship.

Discussion Questions

- What specific adult barriers (e.g., time scarcity, fear of rejection, the "needing others is weakness" mindset) do you personally face most often when it comes to building or deepening your friendships?

- The chapter advocates for cultivating consistent "touchpoints". What is one small, regular action you could realistically take to maintain a stronger connection with a friend?

- The chapter discusses practicing proactive empathy. How can you check in with a friend in a way that opens the door for a real conversation, going beyond a simple "How's it going?"?

- Friendship is described as a two-way street of offering and accepting support. Which do you find more difficult, and why?

Chapter 8: Adventure as a Way of Life

There's a profound difference between escaping your life and stepping outside of it long enough to remember who you are. The first is about running away; the second is about coming home to yourself. For years, I was a runner. My escape routes were varied in the digital worlds of video games, the relentless pursuit of another degree, the grueling shifts on the ambulance that allowed me to focus on anyone's pain but my own. These were all desperate, unconscious attempts to outrun the relentless noise in my own head. It took me a long time to learn that you can't run from a storm that's inside of you. The only way out is to walk through it, one deliberate step at a time.

That's what adventure has become for me. It is not a checklist of exotic locations or a way to flex on social media, but something far more human, more essential. It is a practice of presence, curiosity, and a deliberate disruption of the mundane. It's about breaking the relentless cycle of survival mode long enough to feel the pulse of your own life again. For men, especially those of us conditioned to suppress our emotions, adventure can be one of the few socially acceptable portals to feeling something real again and to experiencing awe, challenge, and even fear, in a way that feels productive rather than paralyzing. For me, it has saved my mental health more times than I can count.

Before I truly understood its power, my life was a relentless state of "survival mode". It wasn't a temporary state of crisis; it was my default setting. It felt like I was constantly treading water in the deep end, my arms and legs burning with exhaustion, just trying to keep my head above the surface. My mind was a thick fog, heavy with the accumulated weight of anxiety, unaddressed trauma, and the grinding financial pressure I carried every day. My internal state was one of perpetual tension, a low-grade hum of dread and inadequacy that whispered, "You're not doing enough, you're not enough".

I was physically present for my family, for my job, for my life, but my spirit felt trapped, suffocated by the relentless demands and my own internal struggles. A typical Tuesday would be a masterclass in this disconnection. I'd be in my classroom, trying to explain a concept to a student, and my mind would be a thousand miles away, running a frantic inventory of bills that were due. I'd be on the soccer field, coaching a drill, but instead of seeing the game, I'd be replaying a tense conversation with my wife from that morning. I'd be sitting at the dinner table, my children telling me about their day, and I would nod and smile while a silent, looping track of self-criticism and worry played in my head. I was a ghost in my own life, haunting the spaces where I was supposed to be living.

The change didn't come from a grand plan or a dramatic resolution. It started small. It started out of sheer desperation, a need to simply breathe air that didn't feel heavy with obligation. It started with simple hikes with the kids on a Saturday morning, a way to get us out of the house and away from screens. It started with spur-of-the-moment detours to dusty state parks we'd spot on road signs during a long drive. It started with wandering through local trails without a destination or driving into a small town we'd never been to and just… walking.

I didn't know it at the time, but I was practicing "microadventures," a concept popularized by British adventurer and author Alastair Humphreys, who defines them as "short, simple, cheap, yet still challenging, refreshing and rewarding" experiences that are accessible to everyone. Humphreys' core message is that you don't need to "fly to the other side of the planet to find wilderness and adventure"; you just need to change your mindset and open your eyes to the possibilities in your own backyard. It's a rebellion against the notion that adventure has to be expensive, time-consuming, and reserved for an elite few. It's a democratization of wonder.

These short, local bursts of novelty did something for me that nothing else could: they snapped me out of survival mode. The shift was immediate and palpable. One moment, I'd be completely consumed by the mental noise, the endless to-do lists, the financial worries, the echoes of past failures. The next, as my feet hit a dirt path or my eyes caught the unexpected beauty of a hidden waterfall, it was like a circuit breaker flipped inside my brain. The noise would quiet down. The relentless churn of self-doubt would recede. A sense of lightness would wash over me, a clarity I rarely found indoors. It wasn't a permanent fix, but it was a vital and necessary reset. My shoulders would physically drop, my breath would deepen, and for a few precious hours, I'd feel genuinely alive again, not just surviving.

I remember one particular unplanned adventure that crystallized this for me. We were driving through rural Georgia, heading home from a family visit. The car was a pressure cooker of exhaustion and irritation. We were all tired, the kids were bickering in the back seat over a dropped toy, and my mind was already on the mountain of laundry and work waiting for me at home. I was in full-on survival mode, my only goal to get home as quickly as possible so I could begin the relentless task of preparing for another week on the grind.

Then my youngest spotted a small, unmarked wooden sign for a "Scenic Overlook," half-hidden by overgrown kudzu. My first instinct, the instinct of the grind, was to keep driving. We don't have time for this. It's probably nothing anyway. The kids will just complain. But something else, a quieter voice, nudged me. It was the part of me that was suffocating, the part that was desperate for just one moment that wasn't scheduled or optimized. "Let's go," I heard myself say, the words surprising me as much as anyone else.

We pulled off onto a gravel road that wound through a dense forest. The air immediately felt cooler, cleaner. We parked and followed a faint path, and as the sounds of the highway faded behind us, they were replaced by the gentle rustle of leaves and the complex symphony of birdsong. We emerged onto a rocky outcrop overlooking a vast, green valley, a river snaking through it like a silver ribbon. The sun was just beginning to set, painting the sky in impossible hues of orange and purple. My kids, who had been at each other's throats moments before, stood silent, their mouths wide open in wonder.

In that moment, the "noise" of my life, the deadlines, the bills, the lingering anxieties were completely silenced. It was replaced by a profound sense of wonder, a feeling of being a tiny, insignificant part of something vast and beautiful. It was a moment of pure, unadulterated awe. This experience of awe is one of the most powerful medicines nature offers. Research shows that awe literally shifts our neurophysiology; it is associated with reduced inflammation, increased oxytocin (the "bonding hormone"), and a diminished focus on the self. An amplified focus on the self is linked to nearly every mental health struggle, from depression to anxiety. Awe pulls us out of our heads and into the present moment, interrupting the cycle of rumination and reminding us that joy and beauty exist, even when we're not looking for them.

That moment on the overlook taught me something profound: healing doesn't happen in a therapist's office alone. It happens on dirt paths, around campfires, or while climbing a rock you didn't think you could climb. It happens when you break your routine and let the world surprise you again.

The science behind this is undeniable. Exposure to nature has been shown to significantly reduce levels of cortisol, our body's primary stress hormone, while lowering our blood pressure and heart rate. This shifts our body from a stressed-out "fight-or-flight" state to a more relaxed "rest and digest" state. This deep, evolutionary connection we have with nature, what biologist E. O. Wilson famously called "biophilia," suggests that time in nature isn't just a pleasant pastime; it's a fundamental human need that, when met, promotes psychological well-being. And you don't need to climb Everest to feel it; studies show that even a 20-minute walk in an urban park can trigger these significant benefits.

For my family, adventure has also become a form of leadership training. It teaches my kids resilience in a way that no classroom or screen ever could. I've seen it firsthand. My youngest daughter, usually hesitant with new physical challenges, once faced a particularly steep and rocky section of a trail. Her face was streaked with tears of frustration, and she wanted to give up. Instead of carrying her or telling her it was okay to quit, I knelt down, looked her in the eye, and said, "You've got this. One step at a time. I'm right here". She grumbled, but she kept going. When she reached the top, the look of triumph on her face was pure, unadulterated pride. That wasn't just a hike; it was a lesson in perseverance. My youngest, who loves to explore, once got completely covered in mud trying to cross a stream. Instead of getting upset, he laughed, embraced the mess, and figured out a new way across. These aren't just fun stories; they are moments where my children learn problem-solving, adaptability, and self-trust in real-time.

When a father, actively healing himself through adventure, engages his children in these experiences, he is not just teaching them; he is modeling a new kind of strong. It becomes a powerful tool for intergenerational well-being, a form of legacy building that creates a healthier foundation for his children and actively breaks the cycle of the "father wound". This practice also strengthens marriage. My wife and I, like many couples, can get caught in the "routine trap," where our days are so full of work, kids, and household chores that our conversations become more about logistics than dreams. But when we step onto a trail or explore a new city on foot, something shifts. I remember one particular hike when we were both feeling the strain of a stressful week. We started out quiet and tense. But as we climbed, the conversation slowly shifted from work frustrations to shared memories, then to hopes for the future. By the time we reached the summit, the tension had melted away. It wasn't about solving a problem; it was simply being together in a new way. Research consistently shows that couples who engage in shared leisure activities report higher levels of marital satisfaction and communication.

For men stuck between expectations and exhaustion, adventure breaks the pattern. It invites us to play again. To get lost and find something new. To test ourselves, but also to receive, to surrender to the moment and be nourished by the world. It's an antidote to the grind mentality that constantly demands output. You don't have to be rich. You don't need perfect gear. You just need the willingness to go. Adventure isn't an escape. It's an invitation to be fully human. This lesson was never clearer than the first time I took my two youngest kids camping by ourselves. The excitement was electric. I had set up our new tent with a satisfying competence, and the kids explored the campsite with a wide-eyed wonder that made me feel like the best dad in the world. This, I thought, was a perfect core memory in the making. But as dusk settled, so did a light drizzle. "No problem," I told them, "this will be a cozy adventure." We huddled inside the tent, the pitter-patter of rain on the nylon a soothing rhythm. Then came the first, slow drip near the corner. Then another near my sleeping bag. Within twenty minutes, "cozy" had turned into a frantic game of Whac-A-Mole, as my wife and I tried to strategically place tape to stop the multiplying leaks.

Amidst the chaos, I pulled out my phone, a knot of dread forming in my stomach. The weather app, which had promised a clear night just hours before, now glowed with an ominous patch of red and yellow moving directly over us. A severe thunderstorm warning. The feeling of failure was immediate and immense; I couldn't even manage one simple night in a tent. My wife and I looked at each other, and the decision was unspoken but clear. "Okay team," I announced, trying to keep my voice steady, "new adventure! We have to race the storm and get everything packed up. Let's go!" And then, something amazing happened. Instead of tears or complaints, my kids' eyes lit up. They scrambled out of the tent into the downpour and started grabbing their sleeping bags, laughing as the rain plastered their hair to their foreheads. They weren't seeing a failed trip; they were living a thrilling escape mission. Watching my four-year-old son, soaking wet but grinning from ear to ear as he dragged a pillow twice his size toward the car, I realized my definition of success had been all wrong. The goal was never the perfect, peaceful night under the stars. The goal was this: my family, working together, laughing in the face of a chaotic, unexpected challenge, and coming out the other side soaked, exhausted, but completely united.

The Microadventure Playbook: Simple Ideas for Deeper Connection

Microadventures are about injecting novelty, presence, and connection into your everyday life without requiring extensive planning, travel, or expense. They are accessible tools for healing, bonding, and a mental reset. Here are some ideas:

With Your Friends (Brotherhood in the Wild):

- **Local Trail Walk & Talk**: Instead of meeting at a bar, pick a local trail. The goal isn't distance or speed, but shared movement and conversation, allowing for a more natural, "shoulder-to-shoulder" connection.

- **Backyard Fire Pit**: A simple, low-cost way to create a relaxed atmosphere. Gather around a fire, share stories, or simply enjoy the quiet. The darkness and warmth can encourage deeper, more honest conversation.

- **Explore a New Neighborhood on Foot**: Pick a part of your city you don't know well. Just wander, explore local shops, and grab a snack. The shared discovery can be a powerful bonding experience.

With Your Partner (Reconnecting on the Trail):

- **Sunrise/Sunset Watch**: Find a local spot with a good view like a hill, a lake, a quiet park and simply watch the sunrise or sunset together. Leave your phones in the car. The shared, silent moment of awe can be incredibly connecting.

- **Backyard Campout**: Pitch a tent in your own backyard. Tell stories, look at the stars, and enjoy the novelty of sleeping outdoors, even if it's just steps from your back door. It's a simple way to break the routine.

- **"Coffee Shop Adventure"**: Instead of going to your usual spot, drive to a coffee shop in a town 30-60 minutes away. Enjoy the drive, the new scenery, and the simple pleasure of a new environment together.

With Your Kids (Leading the Next Generation):

- **Nature Scavenger Hunt**: Create a simple list of things to find (a smooth rock, a specific leaf shape, something red) in a local park or even your own backyard. This encourages observation and engagement with the natural world.

- **Creek Stomp & Rock Skipping**: Find a shallow, safe creek or stream and just play in the water. Skip rocks, build small dams, or look for interesting pebbles. It's simple, often messy fun that fosters presence and connection.

- **Night Walk with Flashlights**: Explore your neighborhood safely after dark, listening to the new sounds and seeing familiar places in a new light. The novelty of the dark can be exciting and a great bonding experience.

Discussion Questions

- The author redefines adventure as "presence, curiosity, and disruption". How does this definition compare to your previous understanding of adventure? What "microadventures" could you integrate into your weekly routine?

- The chapter details the scientific benefits of spending time in nature. How do you personally feel when you spend time outdoors? What specific physiological or psychological shifts do you notice in yourself?

- The author uses adventure as "leadership training" for his kids. What specific life skills (e.g., resilience, problem-solving, self-trust) do you hope to model for your children or other young people in your life through shared experiences?

- Review the "Microadventure Playbook". Choose one idea from each category (friends, spouse/partner, kids/family) that you feel is most achievable for you to try in the next month. What is one small step you can take today to make it happen?

Chapter 9: The Father Wound, the Dad I Want to Be, and the Legacy I Hope to Leave

Fatherhood has been the most important and defining role of my life. It has also been, without a doubt, one of the hardest. There's no contradiction in that statement; it is simply the unfiltered truth of being a parent. It is the only job where the stakes are absolute, where your heart is walking around outside of your body, and where the potential for profound joy and deep, lasting regret live side-by-side every single day.

I became a young dad at eighteen, and my daughter was born directly into a storm of uncertainty, with me standing right in the center of it. I had no roadmap, no money, and certainly no wisdom. All I had was love and fear in equal, overwhelming measure. I never hesitated to step up and be a father but stepping up didn't mean I knew what the hell I was doing. I did my best, but my best back then was often filtered through a lens of my own anger, depression, and a profound emotional immaturity that I didn't have the language to name.

My emotional immaturity manifested in countless ways during those early years. I was quick to anger, not at my daughter, but at myself and the crushing circumstances that surrounded us. A spilled drink, a toddler's tantrum, a late bill, these small, everyday stressors would trigger an internal explosion of frustration that I couldn't contain. I'd snap, or withdraw into a sullen silence, creating a tense atmosphere that my young daughter undoubtedly absorbed into her little body. I remember one evening, she was about two, and she knocked a glass of juice off her highchair tray. The purple liquid splashed across the floor we could barely afford to rent. I didn't yell at her, but a hot surge of rage went through me. I slammed the dishrag on the counter and muttered, "For Christ's sake," under my breath. My daughter, who had been about to cry over the spilled juice, went completely still and silent, her eyes wide with fear that it was not about the juice anymore. It was about me. The look on her face, that flicker of fear directed at her own father still haunts me to this day and she is now 21. It was the moment I realized my internal storm was no longer just mine; it was now raining down on her. I shamefully admit, I have seen that look multiple times in her young life.

I was physically present. I changed the diapers, I did the feedings, I played with her on the floor. But my mind was often a million miles away, consumed by my anxieties and the constant, grinding hum of "not good enough". I struggled to connect with her emotionally, to truly see her feelings, because I was so completely disconnected from my own. I would offer clumsy solutions to her distress instead of comfort, or I would simply shut down when faced with her big emotions, mirroring the emotional absence I had experienced myself as a boy. We still had our own things that kept us close over the years. We had countless daddy-daughter dates, that she might not remember all of them, but I do.

Even now, all these years later, I sometimes lie awake in the dark, replaying moments, conversations, and silences from her childhood. I see all the ways I feel like I fell short, all the emotional needs I couldn't meet because I didn't even know how to meet my own. The guilt from that time is a heavy cloak I still carry. Was my love enough to outweigh the damage I caused? The process of self-forgiveness is ongoing, a daily practice of looking back at that scared kid with compassion and recognizing that he was doing the best he could with the broken tools he was given. It's the daily work of understanding that my intentions were pure, even if my execution was flawed, and accepting that while I can't change the past, I can show up differently today.

I was there physically. I never ran. I showed up, I protected, I provided, I tried. But being there physically and being there emotionally are two vastly different things. I have failed at the second more times than I can count. It's not because I didn't want to be emotionally available; it's because I didn't know how. No one had ever shown me.

The term "father wound" is a heavy one. It conjures images of overt abuse, of angry, absent men who left holes in the hearts of their children. It speaks of neglect, of abandonment, of a loud and clear message that you were not wanted. But my father wound is quieter than that. It's more confusing. It is a wound inflicted not by a lack of love, but by the very nature of that love itself, a love expressed through a relentless, punishing sacrifice that I hated as a boy but have come to understand with the aching clarity of a man who now sees his own reflection in the mirror.

My dad was an awesome father. I need to say that from the start, because the story I'm about to tell is not one of a bad man. He was a good man. A great one. I never for a single second of my childhood questioned whether he loved my sisters and me. We were the center of his universe, the entire reason for the immense, crushing weight he carried on his shoulders every single day.

Some of my best childhood memories are wrapped up in the glow of the television screen at seven o'clock on a weeknight. If my dad was lucky enough to get home from work before we finished dinner, it meant we could watch Jeopardy! together. He would sit in his worn-out armchair, exhausted from a day I couldn't yet comprehend, and he would come alive. He knew everything. State capitals, obscure moments in world history, literary references, scientific principles. He'd shout the answers at the screen before the contestants could even buzz in, a look of fierce, joyful pride on his face. My sisters and I would sit on the floor, mesmerized, not by the show, but by him. In those thirty minutes, he wasn't a tired man drowning in paperwork; he was a titan, a genius. He was our hero.

And he was emotionally there. When I was scared, he was a mountain of safety. When I needed help with a school project, he would put aside his own work, his brow furrowed in concentration as he helped me build a working manual catapult to launch tennis balls for a school project.

He listened. He was supportive. He was present in a way that so many of my friends' fathers weren't. The wound, then, was not one of emotional vacancy. It was a wound of physical absence, an absence so profound and constant that it shaped the very atmosphere of our home.

He just wasn't around.

He worked from before the sun came up until long after it went down. His physical presence in our lives was measured in fleeting moments, the Jeopardy! half-hour, a weekend afternoon if he wasn't called in, a weary smile as he walked in the door just as we were getting ready for bed. He missed parent-teacher conferences. He missed baseball games where I finally got a hit. He missed school events and birthday parties. I remember the ache of scanning the crowd from the pitcher's mound or the stage, my eyes searching for his face, and the familiar, sinking feeling of realizing, once again, that he wasn't there.

As a boy, I hated it. It felt like a choice he was making, a choice to prioritize his work over us. It felt like a rejection. I couldn't understand why the father who was so loving and present when he was home would choose to be gone so much. The anger I felt was a hot, confusing ball in my chest. I didn't have the words for it, but the feeling was clear: Why isn't being with us enough for you?

Now, I understand. God, do I understand. He wasn't choosing his work over us. He was choosing his work for us. His absence was his form of presence. His sacrifice was his love language. And the reason for that sacrifice was the other, darker inheritance he gave me: a crippling, all-consuming anxiety about money.

The tension in our home wasn't from a lack of love; it was from a lack of money. My dad was perpetually, desperately stressed about finances. It was a ghost that haunted every corner of our lives. It was in the strained, whispered arguments my parents would have late at night when they thought we were asleep. It was in the set of my dad's jaw when the mail came, his knuckles white as he sorted through a pile of bills on the kitchen table. It was in the rare moments of rage that would erupt from him, never directed at us, but at the world, at the busted appliance, at the unexpected car repair, at the relentless grind that kept him trapped. He was a man drowning in debt, and he was trying to work his way to the surface, one punishing sixteen-hour day at a time.

I remember one night with crystal clearness. I was about twelve. I couldn't sleep, and I crept out to the living room to get a glass of water. The only light was the small lamp on the end table next to my dad's armchair. He was asleep in the chair, his head slumped to one side, still in his work clothes. On the floor next to him was a yellow legal pad filled with columns of numbers, a frantic scrawl of calculations and budgets. His glasses were askew on his face, and there was a deep, weary crease between his eyebrows that even sleep couldn't erase. In that moment, the anger I felt as a boy dissolved, and for the first time, I was flooded with a profound, aching sadness for him. He wasn't a hero at that moment. He was just a man, trapped and terrified, who was sacrificing his own life, his own peace, his own presence with his children, to try and give us a life free from the very fear that was consuming him. I realized then that his anger wasn't at us; it was at his own powerlessness against the grind.

That image is burned into my memory because it is the blueprint for my own life's greatest struggle. I inherited his work ethic, his sense of duty, his deep love for his family. And I inherited his anxiety. It is a poison that has seeped into my own bloodstream, a constant, low-grade fear that I am not earning enough, not providing enough, that I am just one step away from financial ruin, from failing my own family just as he feared he was failing his.

This is the complexity of the father wound for so many of us. It is not a simple story of good dads and bad dads. It's a story of flawed men who did the best they could with the tools they were given. It's a story of inherited patterns, of love and pain being so tangled together that it's impossible to separate them. My father taught me how to love fiercely, and he inadvertently taught me how to carry my burdens in a silence that corrodes the soul.

The work of my adult life has been to untangle those threads. To honor the incredible love and sacrifice of my father while consciously choosing to break the cycle of his anxiety. It has meant learning to be present with my own children in a way he couldn't be, not because I love them more, but because I am trying to build my life on a different foundation. It means when my own son comes to me with a drawing or a good grade, I make myself put down my phone, turn away from my laptop, and give him my full, undivided attention, because I know with every fiber of my being how much that simple act matters.

It means redefining what it means to be a provider. My father believed providing meant sacrificing his time to earn more money. I am trying to learn that providing also means giving my children my time, my emotional presence, my joy. It means fighting the guilt that crawls up my spine when I choose to go to their hockey game instead of taking on an extra coaching gig. It means understanding that the legacy I leave them will not be measured in dollars, but in the memories, we create, in the feeling of safety and unconditional love I cultivate in our home.

This isn't just a theory; it is a choice I have to make almost daily. A few weeks ago, I was deep in the grind, staring intently at my laptop at the kitchen table, trying to untangle a problem with my side business. The numbers weren't adding up, frustration was mounting, and I was completely lost in the world on my screen. I could feel that old, familiar tension building in my shoulders. Just then, my youngest son came into the room, his face a mess of tears and his small body radiating a storm of frustration. He had been trying to make something, but it wasn't working. It was, in his world, a catastrophe of the highest order. My first, automatic instinct was one of pure irritation. That voice of my own father's grind whispering, can't you see I'm busy? It's just a toy.

But then I looked at his face, at his quivering lip and his clenched fists, and I saw not an interruption, but a choice. I saw the map my father had given me, and I saw the chance to draw a new route. I deliberately closed the laptop, the click echoing in the quiet room, and turned my chair to face him. I slid my chair back and opened my arms. He collapsed into my lap, his sobs shaking his small frame. I didn't offer a solution or try to fix the problem. I just held him, rocking slowly, and whispered, "It's okay to be angry. That sounds incredibly frustrating." After a few minutes, his breathing slowed. We moved to the couch, and I put on his favorite cartoon, pulling a blanket over both of us. We sat there for a long time, not saying much, the light from the TV flickering across his face. As the episode ended, he snuggled deeper against my chest, looked up at me with clear eyes, and said quietly, "Daddy, I love you more than anything." In that moment, the weight of the unsolved business problem, the financial stress, all of it just evaporated. That single sentence was a payment more valuable than any invoice. It was everything.

This is the hardest work there is. It's the daily, conscious choice to look at the map my father gave me, a map of love, sacrifice, and crippling silent anxiety and to thank him for it, to honor the difficult journey he walked, and

153

then to have the courage to draw a new route for myself. A route that, I hope, leads to the same destination of a family that feels deeply loved, but gets there by a trail with a little more peace, a little more presence, and a lot less silence.

Actionable Insights for the Trail Ahead

- **Reflect on Your Father's Emotional Legacy.** Take some uninterrupted time this week to consider the emotional patterns you inherited from your father or father figure. This reflection is not about blame, but about understanding your own emotional blueprint. Journal about specific memories, phrases, or unspoken rules that stand out. Ask yourself: "What did my father teach me about anger? About sadness? About success? Which of these lessons do I want to keep, and which do I want to replace?"

- **Identify Areas for Emotional Presence.** Pinpoint specific situations where you want to be more emotionally available for your children. Is it during their meltdowns? When they share their fears? During bedtime routines? Consciously choose one of these moments and make a plan to be fully present. This might mean putting your phone in another room or setting a reminder to "check in" emotionally during that time.

- **Model Healthy Emotional Expression.** Your children learn more from what you do than what you say. This week, practice recognizing and expressing your own emotions in a healthy, constructive way. This could be as simple as naming your feelings ("I'm feeling frustrated about this," "I'm feeling really happy right now") or demonstrating a healthy stress management technique like taking a few deep breaths when you feel overwhelmed. When you share your own feelings appropriately, you give them permission to do the same.

- **Engage in Shared Challenges.** Intentionally involve your children in outdoor activities or new experiences that require problem-solving and perseverance. These shared challenges are powerful opportunities to build their resilience, foster their self-trust, and create lasting memories. Let them take the lead sometimes and allow for productive struggle before you step in to help.

- **Confront Your "Father Wound."** If you identify with the concept of a "father wound", consider taking a courageous step. This could mean seeking support from a therapist or a trusted men's group to process this past pain. Or it could start with simply writing a letter to your father (one you don't have to send) expressing the feelings you were never able to. Acknowledging the wound is the first step to healing it and breaking the cycle.

- **Create a "Legacy Statement."** Sit down and write a single paragraph that describes the kind of emotional legacy you want to leave for your children. What values, emotional capacities, and relationship patterns do you want them to inherit from you? What do you want them to remember about how you made them feel? Refer back to this statement regularly to guide your actions as a father

Discussion Questions

- The author describes his father's "quiet sacrifice" and physical absence born from love and anxiety. What emotional patterns or coping mechanisms did you inherit from your own father or father figure?

How have they shaped your understanding of masculinity and fatherhood?

- The chapter emphasizes being a "present" father. What does "emotional presence" look like in your daily interactions with your children? What is one specific area where you want to be more emotionally available?

- How do your children act as a "mirror," reflecting back parts of yourself that need growth? Can you recall a specific instance where this happened?

- What kind of emotional legacy do you want to leave for your children? How does this differ from what you inherited, and what conscious steps can you take today to build that legacy?

Chapter 10: Marriage, Distance, and the Invisible Load

I have been married twice. The first time was young, fast, and messy. We were kids, thrown into the deep end of adult life, and our marriage was less a partnership and more a frantic effort to survive. We argued constantly and were not right for each other. That marriage broke me in some ways, but it also taught me a great deal. The most painful lesson from its slow, agonizing end was the brutal realization of how much of my own unresolved pain and emotional immaturity I had brought into it. I was a scared kid trying to be a man, a husband, and a father, all while drowning in the silent, chaotic noise in my own head.

The breakdown was a slow erosion of hope and connection. It wasn't one dramatic fight or a single act of betrayal. It was the accumulated weight of a thousand small moments of disconnection, a thousand unspoken resentments, a thousand times we failed to see each other because we were so lost in our own fear and shame. We were two drowning people who, instead of holding each other up, ended up pulling each other further under.

I remember arguments that would start over nothing, forgotten item at the grocery store, a bill paid a day late, that would escalate into venomous, soul-crushing fights about everything. These weren't conversations; they were accusations. We hurled our pain at each other like weapons, each of us desperate to prove that our own suffering was greater, our own burden heavier. I would retreat into a sullen, stubborn silence, my default defense mechanism. I'd shut down, refusing to speak for hours, sometimes days, leaving her to rage against a wall of my own making. It was a cowardly, passive-aggressive way of punishing her, of controlling a situation where I felt completely powerless. It was a behavior designed to protect the fragile, scared kid inside me, but all it did was create a chasm of silence so wide that, eventually, we could no longer hear each other, even when we were screaming.

The most painful part is looking back and seeing how my own emotional vacancy was the primary poison. I was physically present but emotionally absent. I remember my ex-wife talking to me like I was nothing because of my issues and about her fears for our future. I would sit on the couch, my eyes on the television, and offer nothing but grunts of acknowledgement. I heard the words, but I wasn't listening. I couldn't. To truly listen to her pain would have required me to be present with my own, a prospect that felt so terrifying it was unthinkable. So, I kept the armor on, the thick, heavy plating of emotional detachment, and in doing so, I left her completely alone in the marriage with me.

The end came slowly, then all at once. It was a series of quiet goodbyes that were far more painful than any loud argument. It was the night we decided to sleep in separate rooms. It was the day we started talking about our daughter's future as if it were a negotiation between two business partners. The final conversation was almost clinical, a sterile admission that we had nothing left to give each other. When it was over, I didn't feel relief. I felt a profound, cavernous emptiness. The failure I had been fearing for years had finally come to pass, and it was every bit as devastating as I had imagined. It was confirmation of the deepest, darkest message of the hum: you are not good enough.

That failure, however, became a crucible. In the months that followed, in the lonely silence of an empty room, I was forced to finally confront the man I had been. I saw the scared kid who couldn't articulate his needs. I saw the husband who retreated into silence. I saw the man who let resentment fester because he was too afraid to be vulnerable. It was an ugly, painful self-reflection, but it was also the beginning of a fierce, silent commitment I made to myself: I would do the work. I would figure out what was broken in me so that, if I ever got another chance, I could show up as the man I was meant to be, not the scared kid I had been.

My second marriage has been that chance. It has been different, better, and real. My wife is supportive, patient, and a phenomenal mother. She is a steady partner who possesses the incredible gift of seeing the best in me, even when I cannot see it myself. And yet, like all real marriages, it is not perfect. Some days we are deeply connected, laughing at inside jokes, walking in a perfect, unspoken rhythm. Other days, we are just two ships passing in the night, two exhausted co-managers of a chaotic household, juggling kids and schedules and just trying to catch our breath. And underneath the surface of it all is the invisible load, the quiet, accumulating stress and emotional weight that no one else sees.

I carry my portion of this load like most men do: silently. It is not because I do not trust her, but because I have spent a lifetime learning how to bury my pain so deeply that I cannot always find the words for it. It is a habit, a defense mechanism, a default setting from years of being told to "man up" and "figure it out".

The "invisible load" is a concept that refers to the unseen emotional, mental, and logistical responsibilities carried out in relationships. This includes the "Managerial Load", which is the ongoing responsibility of planning, organizing, and coordinating tasks, and the "Cognitive Load", which is the mental effort of tracking all ongoing tasks and upcoming responsibilities. This mental labor often goes unnoticed because it is internal, yet it demands significant mental space. For me, the invisible load manifests as a constant loud mental checklist that always runs in the background of my mind. It includes upcoming bills, car maintenance, the kids' school projects, work, and the unspoken expectations of my various roles. I might be physically present, playing with the kids, but my mind is simultaneously running a silent inventory of everything that needs to be done, everything that could go wrong.

A mundane example brought this into sharp focus. Our washing machine broke down. My wife was stressed, and I immediately took on the "managerial load" of researching new models, comparing prices, coordinating delivery, and scheduling installation. I spent hours online and on the phone, all while still working my full-time job and coaching. I did not articulate the mental energy this consumed; I just did it. The specific thoughts were a relentless loop: "Can we afford this? Is this the best deal? How will we manage laundry until then? Don't forget to call the old appliance removal". I carried it silently because, in my mind, that is what a man does. He handles problems, he fixes things, and he does not complain about the mental effort involved. It is tied to that deep-seated fear of falling short of expectations, of being seen as incapable or weak . My wife, too, carried her own invisible load of emotional labor, planning social events, and managing household logistics, which I was often unaware of until it manifested as her own stress or exhaustion.

When I am struggling emotionally, I tend to withdraw. I grow distant, stay busy, and resent. And then I shame myself for it. She always notices. But even when she asks what is wrong, I find myself brushing it off with a vague, "I'm fine," or "Just tired". The immediate impulse is to protect her from my burden, to not add to her stress, or to simply avoid the discomfort of vulnerability. It feels safer to retreat into myself, to process things alone, even if that processing often turns into rumination and self-criticism. This fear of vulnerability, deeply rooted in traditional masculine norms, often prevents men from expressing their feelings openly, hindering their ability to form deep, intimate connections.

If I am honest, there have been moments where I have questioned if we are still aligned. There have been times I have thought about walking away, not because I do not love her, but because I felt lost in the relationship, overwhelmed by the unspoken burdens and the growing emotional chasm. One such moment was during a particularly intense period of financial stress and my own mental health struggles. I felt like I was failing on all fronts, and the pressure to maintain a facade of strength was suffocating. I looked at her, so capable and seemingly put together, and felt a profound sense of inadequacy. The core fears driving those thoughts were that I was not enough, that I was a burden, and that she deserved someone stronger, someone who had it all figured out. The thought of walking away felt like an escape from the pressure, a way to spare her from my perceived failures. But ultimately, what pulled me back was the deep, unwavering love I have for our family, and the commitment we made to our kids. It was the realization that true partnership means staying, even when it is hard, and that running away would only perpetuate the cycle of avoidance I was trying to break.

Marriage is a marathon. There are no fireworks every night. It is commitment on the days you do not feel connected. It is the willingness to check yourself before pointing fingers and be man enough to admit when you are wrong and say, "I'm sorry." It is choosing to stay when it is hard, especially when it is hard. We have weathered a lot together, including financial stress, parenting challenges, my mental health, her burnout, and the weight of responsibility that never seems to lighten. We do not always handle it gracefully, but we are learning.

Marriage researchers like Drs. John and Julie Gottman have shown that the most successful couples do not avoid conflict; they repair it quickly and consistently. They turn toward each other in the small moments. They assume the best. They try. A recent example of us successfully applying this principle was during a disagreement about household chores. I felt like I was carrying too much of the "managerial load", and it was building into resentment. Instead of withdrawing, I consciously chose to use "I" statements, as Gottman suggests. I said, "I feel overwhelmed and unseen when I'm constantly the one remembering all the household tasks and appointments. I need help with mental tracking, not just physical doing". It was uncomfortable, but instead of getting defensive, she paused. She then used reflective listening, saying, "So, what I'm hearing is that you feel like you're carrying the mental burden of keeping track of everything, and that's exhausting you, even if I'm helping with the physical tasks?". That simple act of validation, of truly hearing my experience, shifted the dynamic. She has always been good at listening. We then talked about specific tasks and how we could share the cognitive load more explicitly, using a shared digital calendar and a weekly check in.

We have our own ways of reconnecting, such as small weekend getaways, laughing about inside jokes, hiking together, and tackling house projects side by side. We remind ourselves that our kids are watching, learning what partnership looks like. We try to model something real, not perfect. Shared leisure activities significantly improve communication and understanding within a marriage. By participating in a shared hobby or working together on an activity, couples develop better communication skills, learn to appreciate each other's perspectives, and build trust. These shared experiences create lasting memories, foster a sense of unity, and reinforce teamwork and intimacy. For my wife, this means playing pickleball.

There are still disagreements. Parenting philosophies do not always match. I forget things. She forgets things. I feel unseen. She feels unsupported. But in all of it, there is still respect and love for the amazing woman she is. There is still a shared goal of building a home that feels safe, not just for our kids, but for each other. The invisible load will never disappear, but when we talk about it, name it, and share the weight, it feels a little lighter. And that is the thing about marriage; it is not about always being on the same page. It is about holding the book open long enough to keep reading together.

Actionable Insights for the Trail Ahead

- **Identify Your Invisible Load.** Take time to consciously identify the unspoken thoughts, tasks, and emotional burdens you are carrying silently in your relationship. What are the "managerial" or "cognitive" tasks that weigh on you that your partner might not see? Try keeping a running list for a few days to gain awareness. This isn't for scorekeeping; it's for clarity. Once you see it on paper, you can decide what to do with it.

- **Practice "I" Statements.** When you feel overwhelmed or resentful, practice expressing your feelings using "I" statements. Focus on your own experience and needs ("I feel overwhelmed when I'm the only one tracking appointments" instead of "You never help with the schedule"). This opens the door for productive conversation rather than defensiveness. This week, practice this with a low stake issue first to build the muscle.

- **Initiate Low-Pressure Conversations.** Do not wait for a crisis. Find a calm moment to initiate a conversation about your internal state with your partner. It could be as simple as, "I've been feeling a bit stressed lately, and I wanted to share what's on my mind when you have a moment". Choose a time when you are both relaxed, not in the middle of a busy task.

- **Schedule Reconnection Rituals.** Implement small, consistent rituals with your partner that prioritize shared presence and intimacy. This could be a weekly walk, a dedicated "no screens" dinner, a shared hobby, or a short weekend getaway. These shared activities strengthen your bond and create new memories, acting as anchors in a busy life. This week, put one 20-minute "reconnection ritual" on the calendar.

- **Embrace Vulnerability as Strength.** Challenge the ingrained belief that showing vulnerability is weakness. Understand that true strength in a relationship comes from the courage to be honest about your struggles, allowing for deeper connection and shared burden. Remember, your partner likely wants to support you, but they cannot if they do not know what you are carrying.

- **Practice Active Listening.** When your partner shares their feelings or concerns, practice active listening. Give them your full attention, ask clarifying questions, and validate their emotions ("It sounds like you felt really alone in that moment"). This models the behavior you hope to receive and creates a safe space for mutual vulnerability.

Discussion Questions

- The "invisible load" refers to unseen emotional, mental, and logistical responsibilities. What specific "managerial" or "cognitive" tasks do you silently carry in your relationship that your partner might not fully see?

- The author tends to withdraw when struggling emotionally. How do you typically respond when you're overwhelmed or stressed in your relationship? What prevents you from opening up?

- The chapter highlights the importance of "turning toward each other" and "repairing conflict quickly". Can you recall a recent disagreement where you successfully applied (or could have applied) these principles?

- What is one "reconnection ritual" you could implement with your partner to prioritize shared presence and intimacy, even amidst busy schedules?

Chapter 11: Finding North: The Unspoken Power of Mentors and Role Models

While healing is an internal journey, we cannot do it without guides. For much of my life, the map I was given for manhood was incomplete, showing only the well-trodden paths of stoicism and self-reliance. It took me years to realize there were other routes, hidden trails that led to more fulfilling destinations. I only began to see them when I encountered men who were walking a different way, men who served as guides, whether they knew it or not. This chapter is about them. It's about the unspoken power of mentors and role models to help us find our own true north.

A mentor isn't necessarily a formal teacher or an elder who sits you down for lectures. Often, it's the man who models a different possibility through his actions. For me, one of my first guides was a senior paramedic only a year older than me. Let's call him Jon. In the hyper-masculine, tough-it-out culture of EMS, Jon was an anomaly. He was one of the most competent medics I'd ever seen, calm under pressure, decisive, and technically flawless. He commanded respect without ever raising his voice. But it was what he did after the calls that truly set him apart.

After a particularly brutal pediatric call, one that left me feeling hollowed out and shaky, I was back at the station, silently scrubbing the rig, my mind replaying the scene on a torturous loop. Other medics would just turn up the radio, make a dark joke, or disappear into their paperwork. Jon came over, handed me a bottle of water, and just stood there with me for a moment. He didn't say, "You'll be okay," or "Don't think about it." He just looked at me and said, "That was a rough one. Make sure you talk to your wife tonight. Don't carry it home alone." It was a simple sentence, but in that world, it was revolutionary. It was the first time a man I respected had given me explicit permission not to be okay, to not carry the burden silently. He didn't offer to solve my problem; he just pointed me toward a healthier path. He showed me that strength and emotional honesty weren't mutually exclusive. Jon ended up not being just a mentor but a really close friend.

Many of us are starved for these positive, emotionally present male role models. We piece together our identity from the flawed archetypes we see in movies, the stoic heroes who never show pain, or the angry anti-heroes who mistake cruelty for strength. When we lack real-life guides, we are left to navigate the complex terrain of modern manhood alone, often repeating the same mistakes as the generations before us. A good mentor doesn't give you all the answers. They ask better questions. They hold up a mirror and help you see yourself more clearly. They offer proof that another way of being is possible.

Another guide appeared at my first school, a man who modeled a different kind of strength, not with words, but with his unwavering presence. His name was Scott, an ROTC instructor and retired Navy veteran. In the chaotic, often emotionally turbulent world of a high school, Scott was an island of calm. He had a quiet authority that didn't come from his rank or his booming voice, but from the simple, unshakeable integrity he embodied. He was a man who listened more than he spoke, whose office door was always open, and whose primary mission, it seemed, was to provide his students with the steady support and love that many of them lacked at home. He practiced what he preached with hard work, integrity, and a deep sense of duty to others. It was a common joke at the school that Scott had more kids than anyone, as he had legally adopted a few of his former students who had nowhere else to go, officially making the family he had already built in his classroom a reality.

I didn't know him well at first, but I saw the impact he had. I saw the way students who were struggling in other classes would stand a little taller when they put on their ROTC uniforms. I saw the way he spoke to them with a respect that they weren't always afforded elsewhere. He was building men and women of character, not just teaching them how to march in formation.

It was during a moment of profound crisis that I saw his character in its truest form. It was that day I mentioned earlier, when I was walking back from making copies and one of Scott's fellow instructors flagged me down, his face pale with panic. When I ran into the ROTC lounge and saw one of Scott's cadets' unconscious on the ground, my EMS training took over. I became a machine, assessing the scene, barking out orders. "Call 911! Someone get the AED!"

Amidst the chaos, as other adults were frozen in shock, Scott was a study in calm, decisive action. He was the one who, without a moment's hesitation, turned and ran down the long hallway to the main office to retrieve the AED. There was no panic in his movements, just a focused sense of purpose. He returned moments later, breathless but composed, and knelt beside me as I worked on the student. He didn't offer advice or interfere; he and the other ROTC instructor just supported my lead, becoming an extension of my own hands, helping to clear the space, managing the other cadets, and providing the steady, silent support that is so critical in an emergency.

After the paramedics had taken the student away, after the adrenaline had begun to recede, Scott came over to me. He put a firm hand on my shoulder, looked me directly in the eye, and said, in his calm, steady voice, "You did good, Robert. You did everything right." In that moment, his words were more than just a compliment. It was a validation from a man I deeply respected, a man who understood pressure and who recognized the weight of what had just happened. He didn't just see my actions; he saw the man behind them.

Years later, after I had left that school, the connection endured. Scott would still check in from time to time with a simple text: "Hope you're doing well." Then, the day of the shooting at my new school, as the news was breaking and the world felt like it was ending, my phone buzzed with a message. It was from Scott. It just said, "I saw the news. I know you're in there. Just tell me you're okay when you can." Of all the messages I received that day, his was one of the ones that cut through the noise. It was from a man who knew trauma, who understood the unique hell of being a protector in a place that has been violated. He wasn't offering platitudes; he was offering presence, a quiet signal that I was not alone in the darkness. Scott was, and is, a North Star.

Finding these guides requires a shift in perspective. It's about learning to see the mentorship that is already around you and having the courage to seek it out. It might be the older man at the gym who shows up consistently, not to build a perfect body, but for the simple discipline and peace it brings him. It might be the colleague at work who navigates a stressful meeting with integrity and calm instead of aggression. It might be a historical figure you read about whose life offers a blueprint for resilience and purpose. These men are your North Stars. They are the fixed points you can navigate by when you feel lost in the woods.

Identifying these men in your own life is a powerful first step. Think about the men you admire. What specific qualities do they possess? Is it their patience with their kids? Their quiet integrity? The way they listen more than they speak? By naming these qualities, you are creating a composite sketch of the man you want to become. This isn't about hero worship; it's about learning from the living curriculum around you.

The other side of this coin is realizing that you, too, have the capacity to be a guide for someone else. Perhaps the most powerful way to solidify your own healing is to help another man on his journey. This doesn't mean you need to have it all figured out. It just means you need to be one or two steps ahead on a particular trail. You can be a mentor by coaching your kid's sports team and focusing on character as much as on winning. You can be a mentor by being the guy at work who asks a struggling colleague, "Hey, you seem like you've got a lot on your plate. Want to grab a coffee?" You can be a mentor by being the first in your friend group to admit you're struggling, giving others the permission to do the same.

In my own life, I've tried to build what I call a personal "council." It's not a formal group, just a handful of trusted men I can turn to for different kinds of perspective. There's a friend who is financially savvy and can talk me off the ledge when I'm panicking about bills. There's another who is a phenomenal, patient father who I can call when I feel like I'm failing with my own kids. There's a third who is my adventure buddy, the one who will always say yes to a hike that will clear my head. None of them have all the answers, but together, they provide a network of support, a web of strength that is far more resilient than any armor I could ever wear alone. You don't need a guru. You just need a council. You need men who can help you find north.

Actionable Insights for the Trail Ahead

- **Identify Your "North Stars."** Take sometime this week to identify three men, past or present, in your life or that you've read about, who model a quality of manhood you admire. It could be a teacher's patience, a grandfather's integrity, or a friend's emotional honesty. Write down their names and the specific quality they embody. This is the first step in creating your own map.

- **Seek a "Shoulder-to-Shoulder" Conversation.** Think of a man you respect who is a little further down the trail than you are. This week, invite him to do a "shoulder-to-shoulder" activity, grab a coffee, help you with a project in the garage, and go for a walk. Don't go in with a formal agenda. Just create the space for a natural conversation to unfold.

- **Practice Micro-Mentorship.** You don't have to sign up for a formal program to be a mentor. This week, find one small opportunity to be a guide for a younger man in your life. It could be offering a word of encouragement to a younger colleague, genuinely listening to your son or nephew without trying to fix his problem, or sharing a small, relevant struggle of your own to let him know he's not alone.

- **Build Your Council.** Get out a piece of paper and write down the key areas of your life where you feel you need guidance (e.g., Fatherhood, Career, Marriage, Finances, Health). Next to each category, write down the name of one man you know who you feel handles that area well. This is the beginning of your personal council. You don't have to call them all tomorrow, but the act of identifying them is a powerful step.

- **Read a Biography.** One of the best ways to find a mentor is to learn from the lives of those who have come before. This month, pick up a biography of a man you admire, whether it's a president, an athlete, an artist, or an explorer. Read their story not just for their accomplishments, but for how they dealt with failure, adversity, and their own internal struggles.

Discussion Questions

- The author describes his mentors, Jon and Scott, as men who modeled strength through quiet action and emotional honesty. Who have been the "North Stars" or positive male role models in your own life? What specific lessons did they teach you, either with words or by example?

- The chapter suggests that mentorship is often informal. Can you recall a time when a brief conversation or a small act from another man shifted your perspective or provided crucial guidance?

- What fears or internal barriers (e.g., fear of being a burden, not wanting to appear weak) might prevent you from actively seeking guidance from other men?

- The chapter ends by suggesting that being a mentor is a powerful way to heal. In what areas of your life do you feel you are "one step ahead" and could potentially offer guidance or support to another man who is just starting that part of his journey?

Chapter 12: A New Kind of Strong

Strength is not what I thought it was. For most of my life, I believed strength meant being silent. It meant holding it all in, building a fortress around your heart and never letting anyone see the battle raging inside. It meant not flinching when things hurt, showing up without complaint, and grinding through the pain because that is what men do. This was not just a lesson I picked up from culture; it was an inheritance, passed down through the men in my family with the quiet, unyielding force of tradition. My father did it. My grandfather, too. He was a stoic man who rarely showed a crack in his exterior, and his most common piece of advice was, "A man handles his business". It was not a harsh statement, but it carried the immense weight of an unspoken rule: you handle it alone.

The men in my life did not talk about their emotions. They certainly did not cry. They worked, they provided, they showed up, and if they were falling apart inside, that was nobody's business but their own. I saw this stoicism modeled everywhere, by coaches, teachers, and community leaders, and it reinforced the idea that true strength lay in an unyielding exterior. This was the armor I was taught to wear.

I remember a specific lesson in this silent strength when I was about nine years old. I was playing in a Little League baseball game, and I was pitching. It was the bottom of the last inning, bases loaded, two outs, and we were up by one run. The pressure felt immense, a physical weight on my small shoulders. The batter hit a sharp ground ball right back at me. I fielded it cleanly, turned to throw to first base for the final out, and my foot slipped on the wet grass. The throw went wide, sailing past the first baseman. Two runs were scored. We lost.

The feeling of failure was absolute. I felt like I had single-handedly let down my entire team, my coach, my dad who was watching from the stands. As the other team celebrated, I stood on the mound, frozen, tears welling up in my eyes, hot and shameful. My dad walked out onto the field. He didn't yell. He just came up to me, put his hand on my shoulder, and said, "Walk off with your head up. Don't let them see you cry." He wasn't being cruel; he was teaching me what he believed to be a fundamental lesson of manhood. He was teaching me that public displays of pain were a weakness, that the appropriate response to failure was to swallow it down, put on a brave face, and pretend it didn't hurt. So, I did. I bit my lip until I tasted blood, wiped my eyes with the back of my glove, and walked off that field with a stony expression, the sobs caught in my throat like a fist. I learned that day that my pain was my own private business.

But here is the devastating truth I have had to learn the hard way: that kind of strength will kill you. It will not happen with a sudden blow, but with a slow, insidious bleed. It is a false strength that drains you over years of accumulated silence, unspoken resentments, and buried pain. It eats away at your relationships from the inside out, creating a chasm of emotional distance between you and the people you love most. It chips away at your self-worth until you feel like a ghost in your own life. It breaks you down while convincing you that you are doing exactly what you are supposed to do.

This is the central paradox of the masculinity crisis we find ourselves in. It is not that men are not strong; it is that for generations, we have been sold a bad and incomplete definition of strength. Traditional masculinity dictates that men should suppress their emotions, maintain a stoic exterior, and prioritize a rugged self-reliance above all else. These restrictive stereotypes are consistently and directly linked to poor mental health. Behavioral norms like restricted emotionality and the avoidance of anything historically coded as "feminine" act as significant barriers to seeking help and reliably confer a greater risk for depression and suicidal ideation. The very premise of this old model of masculinity is often based on isolation. When men are encouraged to "man up" by internalizing their struggles, they are effectively cut off from the vital support systems of friends, family, and therapy that could provide healing and connection.

So, if that is not real strength, what is?

Real strength is vulnerability. It is the raw courage it takes to walk into a room, look someone you trust in the eye, and say, "I'm not okay," trusting that you will not be judged or abandoned. It is showing up for your wife and being emotionally present when your every instinct is telling you to shut down and retreat. It is sitting with your child in the middle of their emotional storm when you would rather go numb. It is making the hard, terrifying call to a therapist, or having the self-respect to say "no" to something that you know will steal your peace. It is the grueling, necessary work of breaking generational cycles, not just surviving them.

I remember the first time I truly practiced this new kind of strength. I was at a breaking point, the weight of my various responsibilities and lingering trauma feeling unbearable. I came to my wife, and my heart was pounding in my chest. Every fiber of my being, every bit of my old programming, screamed at me to retreat, to put on the brave face, to say, "I'm fine, just tired," which I say often. But I forced the words out, my voice shaky. "I'm really struggling right now," I said. "I feel completely overwhelmed, and I don't know what to do". The immediate internal reaction was a chaotic mix of sheer terror and profound relief. The terror was the fear of judgment, the fear of being seen as weak, the fear of her reaction. But the relief was the immediate release of the immense, crushing pressure of holding it all in by myself. Her external reaction was not what my fear had predicted. There was no judgment, no disappointment. There was just her quiet presence, her hand reaching for mine, and a simple, powerful sentence: "Thank you for telling me. How can I help?". That moment, seemingly small, was a monumental act of courage for me. It was a direct challenge to decades of ingrained silence and a foundational step toward the new kind of strong I was trying to embody.

We have all been shaped by these old models of manhood. Be the rock. Be the provider. Be tough. But nobody told us how to be whole, how to feel deeply, lead gently, or recover from the wounds we have carried since boyhood. When I teach my students about human anatomy, I tell them that the strongest muscles in the body are not the ones that never fail, but the ones that can adapt, heal, and rebuild after being broken down. That is the kind of strength I am learning to lean into. Men everywhere are hungry for new models. Masculinity is not broken; it is evolving.

This new, integrated strength is built on a foundation of Emotional Intelligence (EQ), which is the ability to understand, use, and manage your emotions in positive ways to relieve stress, communicate effectively, and empathize with others. For men conditioned to suppress feelings, developing EQ is not a natural inclination; it is a learned skill that requires conscious, daily practice across four key areas:

- **Self-awareness**: This is the ability to recognize your own emotions and how they affect your thoughts and behavior. For years, I did not have the words for my feelings beyond "fine" or "pissed off". Learning to identify and name my anxiety, my grief, or my shame was the crucial first step toward managing it.

- **Self-management**: This is the ability to control impulsive feelings and manage your emotions in healthy ways. For me, this is the conscious choice to take a deep breath instead of snapping at my kids when I am stressed. It is the strength to set a boundary at work to protect my peace instead of grinding myself into burnout.

- **Social awareness**: This is the capacity to understand the emotions, needs, and concerns of other people. It is the practice of empathy, truly listening to my wife's perspective during a disagreement instead of just formulating my rebuttal.

- **Relationship management**: This is knowing how to develop and maintain good relationships, communicate clearly, and manage conflict. It is the skill of turning toward your partner to repair a conflict, not away from them in anger or silence.

When we, as men, actively cultivate these skills, we are dismantling the armor that has imprisoned us for so long. This process allows us to connect authentically with others, navigate our own complex feelings, and build healthier, more fulfilling lives.

Consider Alex, a successful engineer in his late 40s. He was known for being "rock solid" at work, but at home, he was emotionally distant. His wife often felt like she was talking to a wall, and his teenage son struggled to connect with him. After a health scare, Alex started seeing a therapist who encouraged him to practice emotional literacy. It felt awkward at first. His therapist suggested a simple exercise: each night, Alex would name three distinct emotions he felt that day. He started sharing these with his wife. It was not a dramatic shift overnight, but slowly, by developing his self-awareness, the emotional chasm in his home began to close. His wife felt seen, and his son started opening up about his own struggles. Alex realized that his old "strength" had been a wall, and his new strength was having the courage to take it down, brick by brick.

I do not want to raise my son to believe that his emotions are his weaknesses. I want him to know that he can lead with empathy, that he can cry without shame (when warranted), and that he can be present without losing his power. I want to raise daughters who expect and demand more from the men in their lives, who know that a man's worth is never measured by how stoic he is, but by how well and how openly he loves. I didn't realize how much my own definition of strength had changed until I saw my past reflected in my oldest daughter's life. In seventh grade, she decided to try out for the cheerleading squad. She practiced for weeks, full of hope and nervous energy. When the list was posted and her name wasn't on it, she was quietly devastated. The ghost of my father's voice was right there in my ear, whispering the old script: Tell her to be tough. Tell her it's not a big deal. Tell her to buck up. But looking at her slumped shoulders, I knew that would just be another brick in the wall I was trying to tear down. Instead, I just gave her a hug and said, "I know you're disappointed. You worked hard for this, and it's okay to be sad." I let her be sad. And then I told her how proud I was of her courage just for trying.

A year later, she came to me and said she wanted to try out again. A wave of pride hit me so hard it almost knocked me over. This was it. This was the moment that mattered more than any roster ever could. She knew the sting of rejection, and she was willingly walking back into the arena to risk it again. When the day came and she once again didn't make the team, I braced myself. She got in the car, silent, staring out the window. The old me, the boy on the pitcher's mound, would have seen this as a double failure. But the father I am trying to be saw a victory. I waited a minute, then said, "I know this isn't the result you wanted, and I'm sorry because I know it hurts." She just nodded. "But I need you to hear me," I continued. "I have never, ever been more proud of you than I am right now. Most people would be too scared to try again after being disappointed. You weren't. You showed a kind of courage today that is so much more important than making a team." I watched as something shifted in her posture. She sat up a little straighter. A small smile touched her lips, even though her eyes were still sad. She was still disappointed in the outcome, but in that moment, she knew her father was not disappointed in her. She felt my pride in her character, and you could see that it made her feel proud of herself.

If you'd told the eighteen-year-old me, the scared kid hiding in his own head that one day he'd write a book about vulnerability, he would've laughed and told you to get lost. But here's the truth: real strength isn't in never falling; it's in getting up while still bleeding, looking your people in the eyes, and saying, "I'm still here." And meaning it.

This is how we break the cycle of the father wound. We do not need to abandon masculinity; we need to reclaim it. We need to expand our definition to include the full, complex, messy, and beautiful spectrum of the human experience. Let us be strong enough to say, "I need help". Strong enough to rest when our body and soul tell us to stop. Strong enough to admit when we are wrong, to repair what is broken, and to love with our whole hearts. That is not soft. That is not weak. That is brave. It is time we stop living someone else's outdated idea of what a man should be and start becoming the men we were always meant to be. Strong. Honest. Whole.

Actionable Insights for the Trail Ahead

- **Examine Your Inherited Beliefs.** Reflect on the messages you received about strength and masculinity from your family and culture. How have these beliefs shaped your behavior? Journal about specific phrases or moments that ingrained these ideas in you.
- **Identify Your Emotional Armor.** Pinpoint situations where you tend to suppress emotions or avoid vulnerability. What are the fears that drive this behavior? Recognizing your armor is the first step toward dismantling it. Ask yourself: "What am I afraid will happen if I show this emotion?"

- **Practice Small Acts of Emotional Courage.** Start small. Share one genuine feeling with a trusted friend or partner this week. This could be admitting you are tired, frustrated, or even scared about something. This builds the muscle of vulnerability.
- **Cultivate Emotional Literacy.** Many men lack the vocabulary for their emotions beyond the basics. Find an "emotion wheel" online and use it to expand your vocabulary. Practice identifying what you are truly feeling throughout the day.
- **Reframe Seeking Support as Strength.** Challenge the notion that seeking help is weakness. Whether it is talking to a therapist, joining a men's group, or confiding in a mentor, consciously reframe this action in your mind as a courageous and strategic act of self-care.
- **Model a "New Kind of Strong."** Consider the legacy you want to leave for your children and the example you want to set for the men around you. This week, choose one small, tangible way you can model this new strength. This could involve sincerely apologizing to someone when you are wrong, taking a deliberate rest when you need it, or openly expressing your appreciation and love for

someone in your life. Your actions are the most powerful lessons you can teach.

Discussion Questions

- The chapter argues that "silent strength" can "bleed you dry". How has suppressing emotions or avoiding vulnerability impacted your own relationships or your sense of self-worth?
- What is one small act of emotional courage you could practice this week, for example, admitting a struggle, expressing a genuine feeling, or setting a boundary? What makes this act feel courageous or risky for you?
- Which of the four key Emotional Intelligence (EQ) skills (self-awareness, self-management, social awareness, relationship management) do you feel is your strongest, and which could you focus on developing?
- The chapter states, "We don't need to abandon masculinity. We need to reclaim it". What does "reclaiming masculinity" mean to you personally, and what aspects of a "new kind of strong" do you most want to embody in your life?

Chapter 13: Integration – The Adventure of Becoming Whole Again

There is a moment on every long hike when you stop checking your GPS. You have been walking long enough, breathing in the landscape, paying attention to the creak of your boots on the trail and the rhythm of your own breath, that you no longer need to obsess over the route. The frantic, anxious energy of the first few miles, the constant worry about wrong turns, the mental calculation of distance remaining, and the fear that you are not moving fast enough, begins to subside. Your body, finally in sync with the earth beneath it, knows the rhythm. Your senses, long dulled by deadlines and digital screens, are finally awake. You stop worrying about the destination and start noticing, really noticing, where you are.

That is what healing has started to feel like for me. It is not a finish line, not a fix, and not a formula. It is just a journey where I am finally present enough to realize how far I have come. For years, my life was dictated by that frantic, obsessive control. My internal GPS was always on, constantly recalculating, desperately trying to find a route that bypassed the pain, a shortcut to a version of myself that was finally "good enough". Every step was a calculation against a perceived ideal. Now, that energy has begun to quiet. It feels like the difference between running a race with your eyes glued to a stopwatch versus running for the simple joy of movement, feeling the wind on your face and the strength in your legs. It is the profound clarity that comes from letting go of the need to control every outcome and starting to trust the process of the journey itself.

This is the essence of integration. It is not about arriving at a place where all your problems are solved and all your wounds are magically erased. It is the ongoing work of pulling all the disparate threads of your life together. It involves gathering your past pain, your moments of resilience, your friendships, your failures, your wins, and learning to let them coexist without shame. It is no longer compartmentalizing your life into neat, separate boxes labeled "strength" and "weakness," or "the old me" and "the new me". It is allowing yourself to be a man who has suffered and survived. A man who has failed and fathered well. A man who has profoundly doubted himself and still gotten up the next morning to try again.

For most of my life, I believed that healing was about forgetting. It was about moving on, pushing past the trauma, and wiping the slate clean so I could start over. I desperately wanted to erase the parts of my story that felt ugly or shameful: the unplanned pregnancy, the failed marriage, the moments of emotional absence, and the trauma from EMS and the school shooting. I thought that if I could just bury them deep enough, they would cease to exist, and I could finally become a "new" man, unburdened and unblemished by the past.

I remember sitting in my therapist's office early on, explaining this desire. I told him about the scared eighteen-year-old kid trying to be a father, about the weight of judgment and failure. "I just want to be done with him," I said. "I want to put that version of myself behind me for good." My therapist listened patiently, and when I was done, he asked a simple question that completely reframed my entire understanding of healing. He said, "What if the goal isn't to get rid of that eighteen-year-old kid? What if the goal is to go back and get him? To finally give him the compassion and understanding he never got at the time?" The idea felt radical, almost offensive. Why would I want to embrace the part of me I was most ashamed of? But as I sat with his question, I began to understand. Healing wasn't an amputation. It was a gathering.

But I have learned that healing is more about holding than it is about erasing. It is about developing the capacity to hold your brokenness in one hand and your strength in the other and choosing to walk forward anyway. It is a paradox that men are rarely taught to embrace. We are told to be one thing: strong. But true integration means learning to hold the grief of past losses, like the death of my parents, alongside the vibrant joy of the present moment. For me, this means I can now hold the shame of my first marriage ending and the guilt over my emotional absence, and at the same time, hold the profound love and deep connection I have experienced in my second marriage. The two do not cancel each other out; they form the complex, messy, beautiful tapestry of real life.

This might look different for every man, but the principle is the same. It is the man who can hold the pride of building a successful business alongside the shame of a past bankruptcy. It is the father who can hold the fierce, all-consuming love he has for his children alongside the painful memory of his own father's emotional distance. This is the work: not to eliminate the pain, but to integrate it, to acknowledge its rightful place in your story without letting it define your present or foreclose on your future. The work of confronting my father wound, for example, was not a one-time event; it is an ongoing process of understanding how those inherited patterns of silence still try to influence me, and then consciously choosing a different, more open, more present response.

This journey has been defined by a pivotal shift from a habit of self-shame to a practice of self-compassion. For men conditioned to internalize failures as proof of our worthlessness and to view self-kindness as a form of weakness, this is a radical act. But research shows that self-compassion is a pragmatic and powerful strategy for mitigating the negative effects of burnout and building genuine resilience. It involves accepting that failure, struggle, and disappointment are natural and universal parts of the human experience, negating the need to evaluate personal performance against others or ideal standards.

I still have days where the old "hum of not good enough" tries to creep back in, or where the weight of the "invisible load" feels overwhelming. I might slip into old patterns of withdrawal or find myself neglecting the very habits that keep me grounded. The difference is that now, the internal dialogue has shifted. The old voice screamed, "You messed up again, you're a failure". The new, integrated voice says, "Okay, this is a tough moment. You're human. What's the next small step back to the trail?". That gentle redirection is the core of self-compassion in action. Just last month, I had a moment that felt like a test. It was a Tuesday night, and I was exhausted from a long day, carrying a low-grade sadness for no particular reason. I was on the couch, just trying to be still, while the kids were playing. My son started antagonizing his sister, and I asked him three times to leave her alone, my voice getting tighter with each repetition. The third time, he looked right at me, then turned and hit his sister on the arm. In an instant, a hot, familiar surge of rage went through me. "What is wrong with you?!" I snapped, my voice far louder and sharper than I intended. "Go to your room! Now!"

He froze, his eyes wide with a mixture of shock and fear before he burst into tears. It was the same look I'd seen on my oldest daughter's face twenty years earlier, a look that has haunted me for decades. The old shame spiral began immediately. The critic in my head started screaming: See? You're still him. You're still that angry, out-of-control man. You haven't learned anything. You're damaging your son just like you were afraid you would. In the past, that voice would have won. I would have retreated into a sullen, self-hating silence for the rest of the night, leaving my wife to clean up the emotional wreckage. But this time, something else happened. I felt the shame rising, and I was able to just watch it, without letting it take over. A new voice, quieter but clearer, cut through the noise. Okay, you messed up. You were overwhelmed, and you reacted poorly. You're human. This moment doesn't erase your progress. What's the next right step?

That gentle redirection was the crack of light. Instead of withdrawing, I walked to my son's room, knelt down, and looked him in the eye. "Hey," I said softly. "I am so sorry. Daddy is really tired and frustrated, but it was not okay for me to yell at you like that. That was my mistake, not yours. Can we have a do-over?" His lower lip was still trembling, but he nodded. In that moment, I was holding both men in my hands: the one who had just failed and the one who was trying to repair the damage. I was holding my past and my present without the crushing weight of shame. I was integrating.

It is the tool that allows for integration to happen.

I have realized that the goal is not about eliminating pain; it is about having a way through it. And adventure has been my greatest teacher in this. Not just the big trips to faraway mountains, but the micro-ones close to home. A challenging hike becomes a perfect metaphor for navigating a difficult period in my life. The steep climbs, the moments of doubt, and the physical discomfort all reflect the internal struggles I have faced. But reaching the summit, seeing the expansive view, and feeling the quiet sense of accomplishment becomes a visceral reminder that I am capable of overcoming adversity. A quiet moment by a flowing river, observing the water's relentless, adaptable movement, can teach me about acceptance and the impermanence of my own emotions. The vastness of a starlit sky can evoke that sense of awe we explored in Chapter 8, diminishing my focus and connecting me to something larger than myself.

As men, we need more than just coping mechanisms. We need rituals, purpose, and moments that remind us that we are still alive. This journey of integration, this slow process of becoming whole, has had the most profound ripple effects on my family. My improved mental health and emotional presence have directly impacted my parenting. I am now better equipped to model resilience, adaptability, and open emotional expression for my children. I can now sit with them in their big emotions, validate their feelings, and teach them coping skills, rather than retreating or offering dismissive, quick fixes. This creates a healthier foundation for their own emotional development, and it is the daily work of breaking the "father wound" cycle. My marriage has also benefited immensely. My increased self-awareness and my growing willingness to communicate my "invisible load" have led to a deeper intimacy and understanding with my wife. Our shared adventures continue to be powerful tools for reconnection, fostering teamwork and reinforcing our bond.

Integration is not about becoming someone else. It is about becoming more of who you were always meant to be before the world taught you to build your armor. It is an ongoing commitment to growth and self-care, and it is the ultimate adventure. So, if you are reading this, wondering if healing is even possible for you, I am here to tell you that it is. Not through perfection, but through participation. Through the courageous act of showing up for your life, again and again, with honesty and hope. You do not need to be a hero. You just need to be a man who is willing to keep going. That is more than enough.

If you're wondering where to start, don't overthink it. Pick one thing like a call you've been avoiding, a trail you've been meaning to hike, a conversation you've been scared to have and do it within the next 48 hours. Not perfectly. Not heroically. Just start. You'll be surprised how often the first step isn't toward someone else's idea of wholeness, but toward your own.

Picture this: a trailhead at dawn, air cool and sharp. You've got no idea where the path will lead, only that it's forward. You take that first step, not because you're sure you can finish, but because you've decided you're not staying where you are. That's the trail to wholeness.

And when you feel lost again, as we all do, remember this: every great story starts in the wilderness. Yours still has more chapters to write.

Actionable Insights for the Trail Ahead

- **Embrace Healing as a Journey, not a Destination.** Let go of the all-or-nothing expectation of being "fixed". Healing is an ongoing process of integration, where you continuously learn, adapt, and grow. This week, take a moment to celebrate one small victory or bit of progress on your journey, no matter how insignificant it may seem. Acknowledge that setbacks are an inevitable and acceptable part of the path.

- **Practice "Holding" Your Experiences.** Consciously practice holding all aspects of your life, including past pain, present joys, failures, and successes—without shame. This means acknowledging difficult emotions without letting them consume you and celebrating your progress without demanding perfection. Try a "mindful check-in" each day: take 60 seconds to ask yourself, "What am I feeling right now? Can I allow this feeling to be here without judgment?".

- **Identify and Lean into Your Rhythms.** Recognize the small, consistent habits and rituals that genuinely support your mental and emotional well-being. Whether it is an early morning routine, time in nature, or regular check-ins with friends, these rhythms are your anchors when life gets turbulent. Make a physical list of your top 3 to 5 non-negotiable daily or weekly practices that pull you back to your center.

- **Cultivate Self-Compassion.** When you inevitably get off track or make a mistake, practice self-compassion instead of self-judgment. Treat yourself with the same kindness and understanding you would offer a good friend who is struggling. A simple but powerful practice is to put your hand over your heart and say to yourself, "This is a moment of suffering. Suffering is a part of life. May I be kind to myself in this moment".

- **See Adventure as a Metaphor for Life.** Use every outdoor experience, big or small, as a chance for reflection on your own healing journey. Afterward, take five minutes to write a journal about it. What challenges did you overcome on the trail? What moments of awe did you experience? What did the physical journey teach you about your internal one?

Discussion Questions

- Integration is about "holding" all threads of your life—such as past pain, resilience, failures, and wins—without shame. What is one seemingly contradictory experience from your past that you are learning to "hold" in this way?

- The author's shift from self-shame to self-compassion was pivotal. What is one specific way you can practice self-compassion when you get off track or make a mistake?

- How has adventure, whether big or small, served as a metaphor for your own healing journey? What lessons have you learned about yourself through outdoor experiences?

- The conclusion states, "You matter. You are not broken. You are not alone". What is the most important message you are taking away from this book for your own trail ahead?

Conclusion: Brotherhood, Belonging, and the Next Step Forward

Most of us do not need more advice. We need more friends. We need men who will walk beside us, not to fix us, but just to keep going together.

If you have made it to this point in the book, I want to say something very simple but profoundly important: thank you. Thank you not just for reading these pages, but for being open. Thank you for being willing to listen to a story that, maybe in small or big ways, reflects parts of your own. It takes a quiet courage for a man to even pick up a book like this, to admit, even just to himself, that he is searching for a different path.

This book was never intended to be a prescription, a rigid set of rules to follow for a perfect life. It is a reflection. It is what happened when I stopped pretending, I was fine and started telling the truth about who I really was and who I am still, imperfectly, becoming. It is a testament to the messy, difficult, yet ultimately transformative process of healing.

The most important lesson I have learned on this long and winding trail is that real transformation does not happen in isolation, locked away in the lonely echo chamber of our own heads. It happens around campfires, on dusty dirt trails, and in long, rambling phone calls with the few people who actually listen. It happens in the quiet moments when we finally drop the act, shed the heavy armor we have been carrying for a lifetime, and choose the vulnerability of presence over the safety of performance. It happens when we dare to be seen, even, and especially, in our brokenness.

When I think back on the hardest moments of my life like the quiet, insidious hum of "you're not good enough" that started in my childhood, the deafening shame and judgment of becoming a father at eighteen, the cumulative, soul-crushing trauma from my years as an EMT, the raw, helpless terror of surviving a school shooting, the suffocating, relentless weight of financial stress, and the pervasive, aching loneliness that crept into my friendships and my marriage, I now realize that I did not need someone to come in and save me. I did not need a hero. I needed someone to see me in the middle of the storm and say, with quiet conviction, "I am here too".

That, in its purest form, is what brotherhood is. It is not a boys' club. It is not some outdated, macho bonding ritual. It is the quiet, steady, unwavering presence of men who get it. It is for men who have bled, who have questioned their own worth, and who have walked into the woods of their own lives carrying more pain than they know what to do with and have still shown up anyway. It is the shared, unspoken understanding that beneath the bravado, the busy work, and the carefully constructed facades, we are all just trying to navigate our own complex and often treacherous internal landscapes.

The world is not offering men a lot of that right now. We are often presented with a false choice: man up or sit down. Be tough or be silent. But there is a third way, a better way. A way forward that embraces the full, messy, beautiful spectrum of the human experience, a path that allows us to be both strong and sensitive, both capable and vulnerable, both resilient and in need of help.

The Silent Crisis: What We've Uncovered

Throughout this journey, we have pulled back the curtain on the silent struggles that so many men face, struggles that are often hidden beneath a veneer of stoicism and self-reliance. We have seen how the societal pressure to be strong, self-sufficient, and emotionally impenetrable can become a "silent killer," leading to years of hidden pain and fractured relationships.

- We began by examining the first

"Cracks in the Armor," revealing how early life experiences can forge a prison of inadequacy and shame, and how the very armor we build to appear strong can end up suffocating the man inside.

- We then stared into the rearview mirror at

"Trauma in the Rearview," understanding how the "black cloud" of unaddressed pain can linger for years, and how the stigma in male-dominated fields so often prevents men from seeking the help they so desperately need.

We explored the universal wound of grief in

"The Weight of Ghosts," acknowledging the heavy, cumulative toll of loss. We challenged the silent script that teaches men to be the stoic "rock" for others and instead learned that true strength lies in honoring our pain, practicing active rituals of remembrance, and finding a witness to our sorrow.

- In

"Buried by the Grind," we confronted the pervasive pressure of financial stress, exploring how it becomes inextricably linked to a man's identity and self-worth, and we discovered tools to begin the radical act of redefining "enough".

- We critiqued the toxic myths of "hustle culture" in

"Beyond the Grind," championing sustainable habits, meaningful rest, and firm boundaries as essential and nonnegotiable acts of self-respect.

- From there, we ventured into the heart of the

"Brotherhood in the Wild," tackling the male loneliness epidemic head on and underscoring the lifesaving power of authentic, embodied friendship where simple, quiet presence is prioritized over trying to fix one another.

- We then created a practical guide for

"Sustaining Brotherhood," providing a clear-eyed look at the real-world barriers to maintaining deep friendships in adulthood and offering intentional strategies to overcome them.

- We then saw in

"Adventure as a Way of Life" how "microadventures" can disrupt our survival mode, serving as powerful leadership training for our families and an accessible, essential tool for our own individual healing.

- Our journey then turned inward with

"The Father Wound," exploring the critical, generational work of breaking the cycles of emotional absence to become the present, engaged fathers our children need and deserve.

- In

"Marriage, Distance, and the Invisible Load," we navigated the real-world challenges of modern partnership, finally giving a name to the unseen burdens that men carry and emphasizing the hard, daily work of communication, repair, and shared commitment.

- We then explored the unspoken power of mentorship in

"Finding North," realizing that while healing is an internal journey, we cannot do it without guides. We learned that mentors aren't always formal teachers but are often the men who model a different possibility through their quiet integrity and action.

- This led us to define

"A New Kind of Strong," a powerful redefinition of masculinity where true strength is found not in stoicism, but in the profound courage of vulnerability and the practical skills of emotional intelligence.

- Finally, in

"Integration," we embraced healing not as a final destination, but as an ongoing, lifelong journey of "holding" all the parts of our story, the pain and the joy, the failure and resilience without the heavy burden of shame.

Your Next Step Forward: The Trail Awaits

We need more tables where men can talk honestly. We need more adventures that lead us back to ourselves. We need more fathers who show up, even when they are scared. More husbands who are honest, even when it is messy. More friends who text, "You good?" and actually mean it.

If there is only one thing you take away from this book, let it be this: your story is not over. Your struggle is not a sign that you are weak; it is a sign that you have been strong for too long. And you are not, despite what the voices in your head may sometimes say, alone.

Healing is possible. Brotherhood is possible. Peace is possible. But none of it happens without intention. You have to take the next step. No one else can do that part for you.

- That might mean **reaching out to a friend**. Text that old buddy you have been meaning to call. Invite someone for a walk. Be the one who goes first, even if it feels uncomfortable and risky. Most men are just waiting for someone else to break the silence.

- It might mean **going on that hike**. Start small. A local park. A new trail you have never explored. Remember, just 20 minutes in nature can reduce your stress and reset your mind. Use the "Microadventure Playbook" for inspiration.

- It might mean **finally booking that therapy appointment**. It is not a sign of weakness; it is a courageous, strategic step towards understanding your own internal landscape and finding that "crack of light". The hardest step is often the most crucial one.

- It might mean **sitting down with your kid and really listening**. Model the emotional presence you may have never received. Validate their feelings. Teach them resilience through shared experiences. Put away your phone and give them the invaluable gift of your full, undivided attention.

- It might mean saying two of the most powerful and difficult phrases in the English language: **"I am sorry," and "I need help"**. These are small words, but they carry the immense power to repair what is broken and build the deepest kinds of connection.

- It might mean **setting a boundary**. Protect your peace. Say no to the grind that is stealing your energy and your joy. Prioritize your rest as essential, not as something to be earned. Your well-being is not a luxury; it is a necessity for a life well lived.

- It might mean **embracing self-compassion**. When you stumble on this path, as you inevitably will, learn to treat yourself with the same kindness you would offer a good friend. Learn to correct your course gently, recognizing that progress is rarely a straight line.

These are small things, but they change everything. They are the daily acts of courage that, brick by brick, build a life of wholeness.

So, go. Step out. Move forward. Not because you have it all figured out, but because you are worth the journey. And if you ever doubt that, come back to this page and read this again:

You matter. You are not broken. You are not alone.

The trail ahead is waiting. Take the next step.

And I will be walking it, too.

An Epilogue for Those Walking Beside Us

A Note for Our Partners, Our Friends, Our Family

If you are reading this, it likely means a man in your life has been on a journey through these pages. He might have left this book on the nightstand, or maybe he's started talking in a new language, using words like "the hum," "the armor," or "the grind." Maybe he's been quieter than usual, or maybe, for the first time, he's starting to let you see the cracks.

Whatever the reason, I want to speak directly to you. This man has taken a quiet, courageous step. He has been invited to walk a new trail, one that challenges everything he's been taught about what it means to be strong. The path ahead for him is not about becoming a different person, but about becoming more of who he truly is. And as someone who loves him, you are now a part of this journey, too. That is a beautiful, hopeful, and sometimes terrifying place to be.

This book is a man's story, but it is not his story alone. It's a story about the spaces between people. The quiet that fills a living room. The unspoken fears that hang in the air. The distance that can grow even when you're sleeping in the same bed. His journey back to himself is also, in many ways, a journey back to you.

I know, because I live this every day. My own healing is not a solo expedition; it is a clumsy, imperfect, and ongoing partnership with my wife, a shared effort with the friends who have my back, and a legacy I hope to build for my children. I also know that for every step I take forward, it can create uncertainty for those who walk beside me. So, if you're wondering, "What now? What is my role in all of this?", this is for you.

This is not a guide to "fixing" him. He doesn't need to be fixed. He needs to be seen. This is an invitation to understand the landscape he is navigating, and to find your own footing on the trail beside him.

Understanding the Trail He's On

The most powerful thing you can do is to understand the nature of his journey. For generations, men have been taught that their worth is in their performance. Be the provider. Be the rock. Be the one who has it all figured out. To question that, to admit pain, to say "I need help," feels like a fundamental failure. His silence has never been about not loving you; it has been about a deep, ingrained fear that his struggles would be a burden, a disappointment, or worse, confirmation of his own deepest fear: that he is not good enough.

When he starts to take off the armor he's worn his whole life, it will not always be graceful. The man underneath might be scared, angry, or grieving. He might be rediscovering a sensitivity he buried in boyhood. He might be clumsy with his new emotional language. This process requires patience that is both heroic and exhausting.

Your role is not to be his therapist, but to be his trusted companion on the trail. Here is what that can look like:

1. Learn to Listen for the Hum.

You know his moods better than anyone. You notice the shift in his energy, the distance in his eyes, the shorter fuse. You have been living with the symptoms of his "hum" for a long time. When you see it now, instead of reacting to the symptom (the irritability, the withdrawal), try to see the source.

He doesn't need you to silence the noise in his head. He needs to know he's not the only one who hears it. You can create a space for this with gentle, open-ended questions that don't demand an immediate answer:

- "I've noticed you seem to have a lot on your mind lately. I'm here if you ever want to talk about it."

- "It feels like you're carrying a heavy weight right now. You don't have to carry it alone."

- "I'm on your team. We'll figure this out together."

When he does share, your greatest gift is to listen without the immediate urge to offer a solution. The phrase, "That sounds incredibly hard," is infinitely more powerful than, "You just need to do X, Y, and Z." He's been trying to "just do" his whole life. What he needs now is the feeling of being understood.

2. Embrace the "Shoulder-to-Shoulder" Connection.

As we explored in Chapter 4, men often build trust and intimacy not through intense, face-to-face emotional conversations, but by doing things side-by-side. This is your most practical and powerful tool. Don't force a sit-down talk. Instead, invite him into a shared activity.

Suggest a walk on a local trail. Tackle a home project together. Go for a drive. The shared task or movement creates a comfortable space where conversation can emerge naturally. It lowers the pressure and allows him to open up on his own terms. These "microadventures" are not just about escaping; they are about creating the conditions for reconnection.

3. Let Him Be the Leader (of His Own Healing).

It is a natural and loving instinct to want to take over, to manage his healing, to schedule his appointments, to tell him what he should be doing. But this can unintentionally reinforce the very feelings of inadequacy he is trying to overcome.

His journey must be his own. Your role is to support his leadership, not to take the lead. This means:

- **Encouraging, not directing.** "Have you thought about that hike you wanted to do?" is different from, "You need to go for a hike."

- **Celebrating his steps, no matter how small.** Acknowledge his courage. "It took a lot for you to tell me that, and I really appreciate it." Or "I see you making an effort, and it means the world to me."

- **Respecting his pace.** Some days he will move forward; other days he will slide back. Healing is not linear. Let him rest when he needs to. The trail will be there tomorrow.

4. Protect Your Own Peace.

Walking this trail with him will ask a lot of you. You cannot draw water from an empty well. His healing cannot come at the expense of your own well-being. It is not selfish to set your own boundaries; it is essential.

You are allowed to say, "I have the space to listen right now," and you are also allowed to say, "I love you, but I don't have the emotional energy to talk about this tonight. Can we pick it up tomorrow?" You are allowed to have your own feelings about his struggle, to feel sad, frustrated, or scared. Find your own support system, whether it's a trusted friend, a family member, or a therapist of your own. Supporting him does not mean you have to become a container for all his pain.

A New Kind of Strong, A New Kind of Partnership

As he works to redefine his own strength, your partnership will also have the chance to evolve. The goal is not to return to the way things were before. The goal is to build something more honest, more resilient, and more deeply connected.

It will be messy. There will be days the old armor comes back on, when the silence returns, when the two of you feel like ships passing in the night. But there will also be moments of breathtaking clarity, a shared laugh that feels lighter than it has in years, a moment of vulnerability that closes a gap you didn't know how to cross, the simple feeling of holding his hand and knowing, for the first time, that he is fully there.

These are the moments you are fighting for.

Thank you for loving him. Thank you for being willing to walk this path. He may not always have the words to say it, but your presence, your patience, and your belief in him are the quiet forces that make his journey possible. You are a vital part of his story, and your love is the anchor that helps him find his way home.

Reader's Companion – Putting It into Motion

Reading this book is a step. But it's not *the* step. The real work and the real reward comes when you take what's in these pages and run it through your own life.

These aren't "fix it all" prescriptions. They're small, repeatable actions you can actually do, even when you're tired, busy, or don't feel like it. They're the stuff I've had to test myself and keep testing because just like you, I still have days where I don't feel like showing up.

30-Day Brotherhood Challenge

No group text required. No big speeches. Just proof you showed up. The goal isn't to do everything perfectly. It's to start noticing how much you need people and how much they might need you.

Days 1–5 – The Reach-Out

- Call one friend or family member you haven't talked to in months. Keep it under 10 minutes.

- Text a quick photo or memory to someone you miss. No explanation needed.

- Mail a postcard from your hometown — bonus if you make it funny.

- Share a song that reminds you of them.

- Send a "thinking of you" message with no request attached.

Days 6–10 – The Invite

- Ask someone to grab coffee or lunch and keep it casual.

- Suggest a quick walk at a park or trail.

- Invite them to join you for a microadventure (see below).

- Share an event you've been meaning to try (live music, trivia night, volunteer shift).

- Offer to help with something they're working on like yard work, moving, kid-wrangling.

Days 11–15 – The Gratitude Drop

- Write a short note about something you admire in them.

- Send a voice memo telling them what their friendship has meant.

- Tag them in a memory on social media with a thoughtful caption.

- Drop off their favorite snack or drink just because.

- Share a book, article, or podcast you think they'd enjoy.

Days 16–20 – The Real Talk

- Share one real thing going on in your life.

- Ask them how they're really doing and wait for the answer.

- Admit something you're struggling with.

- Tell them a story you've never shared before.

- Ask them to share a favorite memory from when you first met.

Days 21–25 – The Listen

- In your next conversation, ask two follow-up questions before talking about yourself.

- Notice their body language and reflect what you see.

- Don't interrupt (even if you think you have the "fix.")

- Repeat something, they said back to them to show you heard it.

- Say, "That sounds hard," instead of offering advice.

Days 26–30 – The Repeat

- Pick the one action that hit hardest for you and make it a weekly habit.

- Calendar it. Protect it. Don't wait for "when things slow down."

Microadventure Planner

Microadventures are the antidote to "I don't have time." They prove you can live a little bigger without blowing up your schedule.

Ideas:

- **Weeknight Sunset:** Find a spot you've never watched it from. Bring a snack.

- **Kitchen Campout:** Sleeping bag on the floor, indoor s'mores, zero screens.

- **Unfamiliar Street Walk:** 30 minutes exploring somewhere you've never set foot.

- **Library Wander:** No agenda — just follow what catches your eye.

- **Dawn Patrol:** Get up before the neighborhood does and go for a short hike or walk.

- **Memory Re-Do:** Visit a place from your past and experience it differently.

- **$5 Day:** See how much adventure you can create on five bucks.

5-Minute Morning Reset

Because some days, that's all you've got.

1. Step outside, barefoot if you can.

2. Take three deep breaths.

3. Name one thing you're grateful for, one thing you want to let go of, and one thing you want to try.

4. Say them out loud — hearing yourself changes the weight of the words.

5. Carry one of them into your day as an intentional act.

FAQ – Honest Answers

Q: What if I don't have close friends right now?

A: Start smaller. Think in ripples, not leaps. Say hello to the barista. Ask your neighbor how their weekend was. Smile at the person walking their dog. These micro-moments lay the groundwork for trust.

Q: How do I start when I have no time or energy?

A: Shrink the goal. Think of *one text, one walk, one conversation*. Do the smallest possible version of the thing you'd do if you had all the time in the world.

Q: What if my family isn't supportive?

A: You can't force them to want what you want. Live the change in front of them. Let your actions speak quietly but consistently.

Q: Isn't this stuff too simple to matter?

A: Simplicity is the only reason it works. Complicated plans die the second life throws a wrench in them.

Q: What if I try and it falls flat?

A: Expect it. Not every invitation gets a yes. Your job isn't to make it perfect — it's to keep showing up.

Book Club & Discussion Guide

Leader's Tips

- Keep the tone safe and open. This isn't group therapy, but it should be a place where honesty isn't punished.

- Let silence sit. Sometimes the pause is where the real thinking happens.

- Everyone shares, no one dominates.

- Make space for humor, this is about life, not just struggle.

Questions:

1. Which story in this book stuck with you most and why?

2. Where in your life have you been "in survival mode" without realizing it?

3. Which microadventure idea feels easiest for you to try? Which feels impossible?

4. What's one "grind" you're ready to step back from?

5. How have you experienced brotherhood, friendship, or community in your own life?

6. Which chapter felt like it was written for you?

7. If you could remove one distraction from your life for a week, what would it be?

8. How do you want to be remembered by your family and friends?

9. What does "wholeness" look like in your mind?

10. If you took one action from this book today, what would it be?

11. What's one question you'd ask the author if you had the chance?

12. Which chapter would you share with someone else right now and why?

Recommended Reading

Here are a few books and resources that shaped my thinking, challenged me, or simply reminded me that I'm not alone in figuring this out:

- *The Art of Manliness* by Brett McKay — Not about outdated stereotypes, but about intentional living, skill-building, and meaningful connection.

- *Wild at Heart* by John Eldredge — A deeper look at the masculine soul and the adventure it longs for.

- *Atomic Habits* by James Clear — For building change that actually sticks.

- *Into the Wild* by Jon Krakauer — A reminder of both the beauty and the cost of going it alone.

- *The Comfort Crisis* by Michael Easter — On why pushing past comfort is essential to living fully.

- *Can't Hurt Me* by David Goggins — Relentless, raw, and proof that resilience can be built.

References

All for Kids. (2023). *A father's impact on child development.* Children's Bureau. https://allforkids.org/news/blog/a-fathers-impact-on-child-development/

AMN Healthcare. (2024). *Busting burnout: Self-care for high-stress careers.* https://www.amnhealthcare.com/blog/nursing/features/busting-burnout-self-care-for-high-stress-careers/

American Psychological Association. (2021, October 27). *APA survey finds men more likely to have their worth tied to their jobs.* https://www.apa.org/news/press/releases/2021/10/worth-tied-to-jobs

American Psychological Association. (2023, November 1). *Stress in America 2023: A nation recovering from collective trauma.* https://www.apa.org/news/press/releases/2023/11/stress-america-collective-trauma

Anderson, C. L., Monroy, M., & Keltner, D. (2024). Awe in nature, awe in life: A review of awe's effects on meaning, mattering, and well-being. *Psychological Research, 88*(1), 1-17. https://doi.org/10.1007/s00426-023-01871-9

Australian Men's Shed Association. (n.d.). *What is a Men's Shed?* Retrieved July 25, 2025, from https://mensshed.org/what-is-a-mens-shed/

Better Health Victoria. (n.d.). *Anxiety and depression in men.* Retrieved July 25, 2025, from https://www.betterhealth.vic.gov.au/health/conditionsand treatments/anxiety-and-depression-in-men

Bratman, G. N., Hamilton, J. P., Hahn, K. S., Daily, G. C., & Gross, J. J. (2015). Nature experience reduces rumination and subgenual prefrontal cortex activation. *Proceedings of the National Academy of Sciences, 112*(28), 8567–8572. https://doi.org/10.1073/pnas.1510459112

Cacioppo, J. T., & Cacioppo, S. (2018). The growing problem of loneliness. *The Lancet, 391*(10119), 426. https://doi.org/10.1016/S0140-6736(18)30142-9

Center on the Developing Child at Harvard University. (n.d.). *Serve and return.* Retrieved July 25, 2025, from https://developingchild.harvard.edu/science/key-concepts/serve-and-return/

Children's Hospital of Philadelphia. (n.d.). *School shootings*. CHOP Center for Violence Prevention. Retrieved July 25, 2025, from https://violence.chop.edu/school-shootings

Colorado State University Global. (2022, September 12). *Battling burnout and prioritizing self-care.* https://csuglobal.edu/blog/avoiding-burnout-through-active-self-care-practice

Cox, D. (2021, May 24). *The state of American friendship: Change, challenges, and loss.* American Survey Center. https://www.americansurveycenter.org/research/the-state-of-american-friendship-change-challenges-and-loss/

Crisis Text Line. (n.d.). *Financial stress and anxiety resources.* Retrieved July 25, 2025, from https://www.crisistextline.org/topics/financial-stress-and-anxiety-resources/

Dose of Nature. (n.d.). *Research*. Retrieved July 25, 2025, from https://doseofnature.org.uk/studies1

FHE Health. (2021, September 1). *The gender gap in first responder mental health.* https://fherehab.com/learning/gender-gap-first-responder-mental-health

German, L. (2023, December 12). *7 sad but revealing signs a man has based his entire worth around being financially successful, according to psychology.* GEEditing. https://geediting.com/kir-sad-but-revealing-signs-a-man-has-based-his-entire-worth-around-being-financially-successful-according-to-psychology/

Gheaus, A. (2022). The social construction of masculinity. In E. N. Zalta (Ed.), *The Stanford Encyclopedia of Philosophy* (Winter 2022 ed.). Stanford University. https://plato.stanford.edu/archives/win2022/entries/social-construction-masculinity/

Goldstein, S. (2024). *Beyond tradition: The powerful role of family rituals in building resilience and well-being.* https://www.drsamgoldstein.com/resources/articles/general/2024/beyond-tradition-aspx

Halpern, J., Gurevich, M., Schwartz, B., & Brazeau, P. (2009). What makes a man a man? The case of male emergency medical services (EMS) workers. *The Journal of Men's Studies,* *17*(3), 209–225. https://doi.org/10.3149/jms.1703.209

HelpGuide.org. (2024, March 26). *Improving emotional intelligence (EQ)*. https://www.helpguide.org/articles/mental-health/emotional-intelligence-toolkit.htm

Humphreys, A. (2014). *Microadventures: Local discoveries for great escapes*. William Collins.

Hunter, M. R., Gillespie, B. W., & Chen, S. Y. P. (2019). Urban nature experiences reduce stress in the context of daily life based on salivary biomarkers. *Frontiers in Psychology, 10*, 722. https://doi.org/10.3389/fpsyg.2019.00722

In-Session Psych. (n.d.). *How to help your partner understand and take on some of your mental load*. Retrieved July 25, 2025, from https://insessionpsych.com/how-to-help-your-partner-understand-and-take-on-some-of-your-mental-load/

Johnsen, K. C., Raaheim, A., & Alme, T. A. (2017). Emotional state of young fathers. *Social Psychiatry and Psychiatric Epidemiology, 52*, 163–170. https://doi.org/10.1007/s00127-016-1306-3

Keating, D. (2020, October 13). *Toxic masculinity is unsafe... for men*. MSU Today.

https://msutoday.msu.edu/news/2020/toxic-masculinity-is-unsafe-for-men

KFF Health News. (2024, May 17). *Men's mental health affected by financial, societal pressures.* https://kffhealthnews.org/morning-breakout/mens-mental-health-affected-by-financial-societal-pressures-report/

Li, Q. (2010). Effect of forest bathing trips on human immune function. *Environmental Health and Preventive Medicine, 15*(1), 9–17. https://doi.org/10.1007/s12199-009-0086-9

Lim, H. J., & Zeman, J. (2021). Financial stressors, parent-adolescent relationship, and adolescents' emotional well-being: The moderating role of adolescents' gender and parents' gender. *Journal of Family and Economic Issues, 42*, 269–282.

Lowe, S. R., & Galea, S. (2017). The mental health consequences of mass shootings. *Trauma, Violence, & Abuse, 18*(1), 62–82. https://doi.org/10.1177/1524838015591522

Lurie Children's Hospital of Chicago. (2021, June 17). *Father's mental health plays key role in child development, research shows.* https://www.luriechildrens.org/en/news-stories/fathers-mental-health-plays-key-role-in-child-development-research-shows/

National Institute of Mental Health. (n.d.). *Post-traumatic stress disorder.* Retrieved July 25, 2025, from https://www.nimh.nih.gov/health/topics/post-traumatic-stress-disorder-ptsd

Nicastro, R. (2024, November 18). *Childhood trauma and the shame men carry.* https://www.richardnicastro.com/2024/11/18/childhood-trauma-and-the-shame-men-carry/

Number Analytics. (2023). *Ultimate guide to shared activities in marriage and family.* https://numberanalytics.com/blog/ultimate-guide-to-shared-activities-in-marriage-and-family

Ogrodniczuk, J. S., & Oliffe, J. L. (2011). Men and depression. *Canadian Family Physician, 57*(2), 153–155.

Papyrus. (n.d.). *Setting boundaries.* Retrieved July 25, 2025, from https://www.papyrus-uk.org/setting-boundaries/

Patsiopoulos, A. T., & Buchanan, M. J. (2011). The practice of self-compassion in counseling: A narrative inquiry. *Professional Psychology: Research and Practice, 42*(4), 301–307. https://doi.org/10.1037/a0024482

PBS NewsHour. (2022, October 3). *Why a growing number of American men say they are in a 'friendship recession'.* https://www.pbs.org/newshour/show/why-a-growing-number-of-american-men-say-they-are-in-a-friendship-recession

Pew Research Center. (2023, December 7). *Men and women in the U.S. see friendships differently.* https://www.pewresearch.org/social-trends/2023/12/07/men-and-women-in-the-u-s-see-friendships-differently/

Quintilian School. (n.d.). *The role of outdoor education in child development.* Retrieved July 25, 2025, from https://quintilianschool.wa.edu.au/the-role-of-outdoor-education-in-child-development/

Reeves, R. V. (2022). *Of boys and men: Why the modern male is struggling, why it matters, and what to do about it.* Brookings Institution Press.

Seidler, Z. E., Dawes, A. J., Rice, S. M., Oliffe, J. L., & Dhillon, H. M. (2016). The role of masculinity in men's help-seeking for depression: A systematic review. *Clinical Psychology Review,* *49,* 106–124. https://doi.org/10.1016/j.cpr.2016.09.002

Shapiro, J. (2024, January 2). Are you carrying the invisible load in your relationship? *Psychology Today.* https://www.psychologytoday.com/us/blog/social-instincts/202401/are-you-carrying-the-invisible-load-in-your-relationship

Shear, M. K. (2015). Complicated grief. *The New England Journal of Medicine,* *372*(2), 153–160. https://doi.org/10.1056/NEJMcp1315618

Therapy Group D.C. (n.d.). *Understanding male intimacy struggles.* Retrieved July 25, 2025, from https://therapygroupdc.com/therapist-dc-blog/understanding-male-intimacy-struggles/

The Wellness Universe. (2024). *Unlocking emotional intelligence in men.* https://blog.thewellnessuniverse.com/unlocking-emotional-intelligence-in-men/

Threlfall, D. (2023, June 14). How burnout manifests differently in men. *Forbes.* https://www.forbes.com/sites/drdeborahlee/2023/06/14/how-burnout-manifests-differently-in-men/

Triony Behavioral Health. (2023). *The benefits of group therapy for men.* https://www.trionybehavioralhealth.com/mens-mental-health/the-benefits-of-group-therapy-for-men/

U.S. Department of Health and Human Services. (2023a, May 3). *New Surgeon General advisory raises alarm about the devastating impact of the epidemic of loneliness and isolation in the United States.* https://www.hhs.gov/about/news/2023/05/03/new-surgeon-general-advisory-raises-alarm-about-devastating-impact-epidemic-loneliness-isolation-united-states.html

U.S. Department of Health and Human Services. (2023b). *Parenting.* Office of the Surgeon General. https://www.hhs.gov/surgeongeneral/reports-and-publications/parents/index.html

Valentin, C. (2022). Mapping men's mental health help-seeking after an intimate partner relationship break-up.

Journal of Men's Studies, 30(2), 221-239. https://doi.org/10.1177/10608265211051512

van der Gaag, N., Heilman, B., & Barker, G. (2020). *The state of America's boys: An urgent case for a more connected, just, and equal world for and with boys*. Equimundo. https://equimundo.org/resources/the-state-of-americas-boys-2020/

Venture Zero. (2024). *Lifting the lid on men's mental health: What the recent Bupa Wellbeing Index research tells us about workplace wellbeing*. https://www.venturezero.co.uk/post/lifting-the-lid-on-mens-mental-health-what-the-recent-bupa-wellbeing-index-research-tells-us-about-workplace-wellbeing

Vigil, N. H., Grant, A. R., Perez, O., & Calkins, C. (2019). Death by suicide: The EMS profession compared to the general public. *Prehospital Emergency Care, 23*(3), 340–345. https://doi.org/10.1080/10903127.2018.1514350

Waldinger, R. J., & Schulz, M. S. (2023). *The good life: Lessons from the world's longest scientific study of happiness*. Simon & Schuster.

Weller, F. (2015). *The wild edge of sorrow: Rituals of renewal and the sacred work of grief.* North Atlantic Books.

Whitelaw, S., Thapar, A., & van der Merwe, A. (2024). Problematizing loneliness as a public health issue: an analysis of policy in the United Kingdom. *Perspectives in Public Health, 144(1),* 11-13. https://doi.org/10.1177/17579139231221775

Wigert, B. (2020, December 2). *Employee burnout: The biggest myth.* Gallup. https://www.gallup.com/workplace/326889/employee-burnout-biggest-myth.aspx

Wilson, E. O. (1984). *Biophilia.* Harvard University Press.

Workplace Strategies for Mental Health. (n.d.). *Setting healthy boundaries at work.* Retrieved July 25, 2025, from https://workplacestrategiesformentalhealth.com/resources/setting-healthy-boundaries-at-work

Resources for the Trail Ahead

This journey toward wholeness is not one you have to walk alone. If you find yourself needing additional support, the following organizations, helplines, and directories can provide further guidance, connection, and professional help.

Crisis & Urgent Support

988 Suicide & Crisis Lifeline

Offers 24/7 call, text, and chat access to trained crisis counselors for anyone experiencing suicidal, substance use, or mental health crises, or any other emotional distress. You can also dial 988 if you are worried about a loved one.

- **Call/Text**: 988

- **Chat**: 988lifeline.org/chat

Crisis Text Line

Provides free, confidential support 24/7 from a trained volunteer Crisis Counselor.

- **Text**: HOME to 741741

Veterans Crisis Line

- **Call**: 988 (Press 1)

- **Text**: 838255

Men's Mental Health Specific

Man Therapy®

An evidence-based effort to break through stigma and reduce male suicide. Offers a "Head Inspection" tool and therapist finder.

- **Website**: mantherapy.org

Face It Foundation

Provides peer support, group sessions, and resources for men navigating depression.

- **Website**: faceitfoundation.org

HeadsUpGuys

A resource from the University of British Columbia offering tips, tools, and personal stories to help men fight depression.

- **Website**: headsupguys.org

TherapyForBlackMen.org

Provides a directory of multiculturally competent therapists and coaches for men of color. Offers supportive resources.

- **Website**: therapyforblackmen.org

Trauma & PTSD Support

The National Center for PTSD

A leading federal resource for information, research, and education on PTSD and trauma.

- **Website**: ptsd.va.gov

1in6

Supports men who have had unwanted or abusive sexual experiences. Offers a 24/7 online helpline and support groups.

- **Website**: 1in6.org

National Domestic Violence Hotline

Supports people who have experienced any form of domestic abuse.

- **Phone**: 1-800-799-SAFE (7233)

- **Text**: START to 88788

Loneliness & Social Connection

Men's Sheds Association (USA)

Provides community spaces for men to connect, converse, and create through shared activities.

- **Website**: menssheds.org

The Mankind Project

An international nonprofit that facilitates challenging and highly rewarding programs for men at every stage of life.

- **Website**: mankindproject.org

Meetup

A platform to find and build local communities. Can be used to search for men's groups, hiking clubs, or other shared interests in your area.

- **Website**: meetup.com

Financial Stress & Anxiety

National Foundation for Credit Counseling (NFCC)

Offers affordable assistance for managing personal finances and debt.

- **Website**: nfcc.org

Consumer Financial Protection Bureau (CFPB)

Provides accessible guides on managing personal finances.

- **Website**: consumerfinance.gov

Therapy & Counseling Directories

Psychology Today

A widely used directory to find therapists, psychiatrists, and treatment centers by location, specialty, and insurance.

- **Website**: psychologytoday.com

Open Path Psychotherapy Collective

A directory of therapists who offer lower rates on a sliding scale, making therapy more accessible.

- **Website**: openpathcollective.org

Author's Notes

This book didn't happen overnight.

It came together in the spaces between work, family, and the moments I thought about shelving the whole thing. Some chapters were easy since they'd been sitting in me for years, waiting for a reason to come out. Others I had to wrestle with, not because I didn't have the words, but because I wasn't sure I wanted to share them.

There are stories that didn't make it in here. Some because they didn't fit the arc. Others because they still feel too raw. But maybe that's the point, healing is never just one book, one conversation, one breakthrough. It's a string of imperfect attempts, and you hope enough of them add up to something worth holding on to.

What I hope you take away from this isn't that I've figured it all out because I haven't. It's that you're not the only one carrying the weight you carry. That there's a way forward that doesn't require burning yourself out to prove you're strong. And that sometimes, the smallest, simplest steps can open the biggest doors.

If this book has done anything for you, challenged you, encouraged you, or just made you feel seen for a page or two I'd love to hear about it. Because the conversation doesn't end here. It's just getting started.

About the Author

Robert Yadon is a husband, father of three, grandfather, high school teacher, and former EMT who has spent his adult life navigating trauma, burnout, and the quiet weight that many men carry. He's not a therapist, influencer, or polished self-help guru; he's a man who's been to the bottom and is doing the hard work to climb back up, one step at a time.

Through years of struggling silently while showing up for his students, coaching on the sidelines, and raising a family, Robert began writing not to impress anyone, but to survive. What started as an outlet became a mission: to help men feel less alone, less ashamed, and more equipped to take back their lives.

He now writes and speaks with unfiltered honesty about fatherhood, marriage, mental health, and what it means to reclaim adventure, purpose, and peace in a world that rarely gives men permission to slow down. His work is grounded in real-life experiences, practical insight, and a deep belief that vulnerability and strength can coexist.

When he's not writing, you can find him on the trail with his family, coaching soccer, or chasing meaning through microadventures.